THE NUTRIENT AND VITAMIN DIET BOOK

THE NUTRIENT AND VITAMIN DIET BOOK

by Dorothy N. Kent

GROSSET & DUNLAP
A NATIONAL GENERAL COMPANY
Publishers · New York

A Castle Books, Inc. Edition
Distributed To The Trade
By Book Sales, Inc.

Contents

Foreword

Overweight and malnutrition are two of the greatest problems America faces today. Early death, divorce, depression, physical illness and the opportunity to give and receive love can be related to these problems. Yet there is no reason for the vast majority of people to be overweight or malnourished. The computed diet contained in this book can help most people lose weight as well as maintain a nutritionally balanced diet. I recommended it for dieters and non-dieters alike.

—JOHN F. WHISENHUNT, M.D.

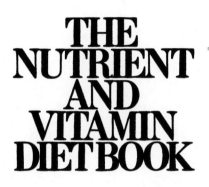

THE NUTRIENT AND VITAMIN DIET BOOK

Why A Nutrient And Vitamin Diet?

WHY A NUTRIENT
AND VITAMIN DIET?

For the past two decades, a variety of spectacular weight-loss diets have inundated the American scene. Some have actually helped people lose weight but most have also caused a nutritional deficiency in their users i.e., the dieters have not consumed the recommended daily nutrient and vitamin allowances needed for good health. The result of these deficiencies is often frustration, irritability, anxiety and illness. With the more bizarre diets, permanent health damage can ensue.

Thanks to government studies, a weight-loss diet can be computed that includes the total amount of nutrients and vitamins needed for everyday good health—the same amounts needed for your ideal weight.

In this book, three weeks of menus and recipes have been computed not only to provide the necessary nutrients and vitamins in your diet but to help you lose weight. Food supplements are suggested with each menu for the non-dieting members of the family. Some of the extra vitamins and nutrients inherent in the supplements can create a "bank" that your system will fall back on when needed for increased activity or in times of physical stress.

In addition, this book contains two bonuses. The first is a crash diet that, as with all crash diets, should only be undertaken with your doctor's approval. The diet presented here is one week of menus and recipes with a daily caloric intake of about 600 calories. The carbohydrate count is low yet the diet is high in vitamins and calcium.

The second bonus is a new approach to cooking vegetables that "seals in" vitamins while greatly enhancing the flavor of the food.

Even with the government tables at hand, the computation of nutrients and vitamins for every meal would be far too taxing and time consuming for the busy meal planner. Thus this book can be a very important tool for both the dieter and non-dieter in achieving or maintaining a slim and vigorous figure, and a guide for the doctor who is dedicated to instructing his patients toward such a goal.

The nine dietary allowances given in the menu section for breakfast, lunch and dinner are deemed sufficient for a balanced daily diet since the foods in which they are found contain the trace minerals: Vitamins B-6, B-12, pantothenic acid, biotin and Vitamins E and K.

The tenth allowance, Vitamin D, is not listed because only 400 International Units are necessary for infants and children up to the age of nineteen and for adults over sixty-five. This vitamin is found in adequate quantity in the menus presented.

Each breakfast, lunch and dinner menu is computed separately to aid every individual in reaching adequate nutrient and vitamin levels each day. If a meal has to be skipped, try to make up for the nutrients and vitamins missed before the day is over. Take a glass of milk for calcium; a hard-boiled egg for protein; tomato juice for Vitamin A.

As shown in the table of Recommended Daily Nutrient and Vitamin Allowances, almost all men need about twenty per cent more protein per day than the average woman. An extra egg at breakfast or a little larger serving of meat (about twenty per cent more) at another meal will be sufficient.

The iron level in the menus has been increased to the suggested allowance and even exceeds it on some days; however, pregnant women may wish to drink a few ounces of fresh prune juice for additional iron. (Fresh prune juice is a new product that is available in resealable glass containers.)

The importance of deriving the necessary nutrients and vitamins from natural sources i.e., food versus pills and tonics, cannot be overstated. In the United States Department of Agriculture's YEAR-BOOK the question is asked:

"*Why can't I eat and drink whatever I please and take vitamins and mineral capsules to make sure I get essential nutrients?*"
"A diet chosen by chance is not safe. It may lack protein and energy and other essential nutrients. It may supply too much carbohydrate and not enough other essentials. Vitamin and mineral preparations cannot take the place of the food sources of nutrients."

RECOMMENDED DAILY NUTRIENT AND VITAMIN ALLOWANCES*

	Calories (non-dieting)	Protein (gm.)	Calcium (gm.)	Iron (mg.)	Vitamin A (I.U.)	Thiamine (mg.)	Riboflavin (mg.)	Vitamin C (mg.)	Niacin** (mg.)
Men: 25-45	3,200	70	0.8	10	5,000	1.6	1.8	75	21
Men: 45-65	3,000	70	0.8	10	5,000	1.5	1.8	75	20
Women: 25-45	2,300	58	0.8	12	5,000	1.2	1.5	70	17
Women: 45-65	2,200	58	0.8	12	5,000	1.1	1.5	70	17

gm. = grams
mg. = milligrams
I.U. = international units

* Source: United States Department of Agriculture Yearbook
** 25% more niacin is needed for each 10 pounds of excess weight. The foods having the highest niacin content are: lean ground round steak, chicken, liver, bologna, mackeral, pink salmon, oysters and shad. Swordfish has the highest niacin content of fish. 1 cup of peanuts has 2 ½ times as much but is more fattening. Dried peaches, apricots and dates are highest of the fruits. Whole wheat bread is highest in cereals.

New Ways
of Cooking Vegetables

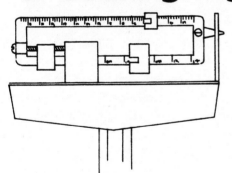

NEW WAYS
OF COOKING VEGETABLES

It has long been known that the use of water in cooking, especially vegetables, accounts for a vitamin loss as well as a loss in flavor. The French had discovered that a paste, of flour and water, used to seal the casserole or pan accounted for an enormous improvement in flavor. The only problems were that the paste often cracked and the steam escaped; it was difficult to clean the utensil after use and it was impossible to check doneness while the dish was cooking. Two alternate methods of sealing follow.

1. THE TAPE METHOD
After experimentation I have discovered that masking tape (with rubber cement backing and crinkled paper

front) will seal any pan or casserole thoroughly. Because it does not get hot or burn, it can be removed during cooking and resealed. A truly wonderful result is obtained: frozen vegetables can be cooked without water; most fresh vegetables with only 1 or 2 tablespoons and fresh summer squash and zucchini with almost none at all. Spinach, cooked with just the water remaining on its washed leaves, becomes a taste delight. In short— vegetables become far more tasty and much more nutritious. Use masking tape that is at least 1 ¼ -inches wide. Wrap the tape carefully around the lid and top edge of the pan, casserole or skillet—press down both tape edges to seal. The tape can be used several times. Simply stick it on the back of the cupboard door for future use.

2. THE FOIL METHOD

Tear off a square of aluminum foil larger than your pan or casserole and place over the top of it. Press the lid down tightly and fold the foil up around the edges to seal. Most of the time this foil can be rinsed off and used several times more.

It will be best to experiment with both methods to find the most satisfactory way to deal with your utensils. Both methods take shorter cooking time than the usual way of cooking but your stove will be the arbiter of this phase. Low heat is stressed in all recipes, since the vegetables, without water or with little water, depend upon their juices to steam to doneness. The following table provides a guide to the water needed to cook specific vegetables.

Vegetables*   Amount of Water

Artichoke hearts, frozen .....*1 teaspoon*

Asparagus, frozen ....*1 tablespoon per carton*

Asparagus, fresh ....*2 tablespoons per pound*

Beans, lima, frozen ....*2 teaspoons*

Beans, string, frozen ....*No water (both Italian and French cut)*

Beans, string, fresh ....*2 tablespoons per pound*

Broccoli, frozen ....*No water*

Broccoli, fresh ....*2 tablespoons (washed with water on leaves)*

Cabbage, fresh ....*1 tablespoon per quarter head (to steam)*

Cabbage, sauerkraut ....*No water*

Carrots, frozen ....*1 teaspoon*

Carrots, fresh ....*2 tablespoons for about 4 large, sliced*

Carrots, baked in foil ....*No water; a little butter and seasoning*

Corn on the cob, frozen ......*2 tablespoons*

Corn, fresh, with husks ......*Wash, clean; rewrap with damp husks, and use ¼ cup water for 4 to 5 ears*

Peas, frozen ....*1 teaspoon (with pearl onions, 2)*

Peas, fresh ....*2 tablespoons*

Potatoes, fresh, steamed ..... *¼ cup water*

Spinach, fresh or frozen .....*No water (fresh has water on its washed leaves)*

Sprouts, bean, washed........*No water. (has enough on sprouts)*

Sprouts, Brussels, frozen ....*No water*
Sprouts, Brussels, fresh ...... ¼ *cup*
Squash, summer, frozen .....*No water*
Squash, summer, fresh ....*1 teaspoon*
Squash, winter, frozen ....*No water*
Squash, zucchini, frozen ....*No water*
Squash, zucchini, fresh ....*1 teaspoon*

*Turn heat to high for 1 to 2 minutes on a gas stove, 2 to 3 minutes on an electric oven, then turn to simmer. For oven dishes, preheat oven to 400 or 450°, then reduce to moderate.

The Nutrient
and Vitamin Diet

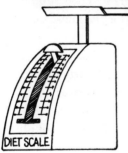

THE NUTRIENT AND VITAMIN DIET

The following diet, consisting of three weeks of menus and recipes, has been computed not only to provide the necessary nutrients and vitamins for each day's good health but to help you lose weight. Food supplements are suggested with each menu for the non-dieting members of the family.

There are three things to do to create a base for your computed diet or crash diet. First: keep a carton of dry nonfat milk on hand. If your family is two or more, keep some mixed in the refrigerator for cooking. Second: stock either canned chicken broth or keep a supply of homemade broth on hand if you have freezer space for it. It is the base for many recipes and adds the all important niacin as well as greatly added flavor. Third: keep a small carton of plain yogurt on hand at all times. It is needed almost every day and keeps well. If water comes to the surface, simply restir.

In the interest of economy and lack of waste, persons who live alone and families of two may wish to repeat one entire day's menu in order to utilize a large can of salmon, a whole chicken, etc. Each day's menus are computed for all the needed nutrients and vitamins but do bear in mind that five green vegetables and two yellow vegetables are needed during a one-week period.

1ST MONDAY

Breakfast

Menu: *Carbohydrates*

Prune Juice, ½ cup 1
Poached or Soft-Boiled Egg, 1 0
Whole Wheat Toast, ½ slice 6
Butter, 1 teaspoon 0
Coffee, Black 0

Nutrients and Vitamins:

Protein 9, Calcium 58, Iron 8.1 ½, Vitamin A
820, Thiamine .20, Riboflavin .23 ½,
Vitamin C 38, Niacin 1.1 ½, Fatty Acids 5

Lunch

Menu:

Chicken Salad in Lettuce Cups
Carrots Sticks
Coffee or Tea with Lemon

Ingredients: *Carbohydrates*

Chicken, boned and diced, ½ cup 0
Celery, 1 stalk diced 1
Mayonnaise, 1 tablespoon 0
Lettuce leaves, 2 1
Carrots sticks, 6 slim ....1 ½
Coffee or tea, plain 0

Nutrients and Vitamins:

Protein 31 ½, Calcium 47.1, Iron 1.27, Vitamin A
2,420, Thiamine .87, Riboflavin .27, Vitamin C 11,
Niacin 10.1, Fatty Acids 15

Dinner

Menu:

Green Peppers a la Florentina
Zucchini Squash
Winter Squash with Butter
Green Asparagus
Coffee or Tea

Ingredients: *Carbohydrates*

Green bell pepper, 1 3
Cheddar cheese, sharp, 1-inch cube 1
Ground round or chuck steak, lean, 1 cup...............0
Egg, 1 0
Parsley, snipped, about 3 sprigs 0
Winter squash, mashed, ⅓ cup ....8 ½
Zucchini squash, ½ cup 4
Green asparagus, 6 spears 3

Nutrients and Vitamins:

Protein 39 ½, Calcium 272, Iron 3.25, Vitamin A
5,670, Thiamine 3.19, Riboflavin 1.46,
Vitamin C 96, Niacin 7.5, Fatty Acids 7

Method:

Cut top from green pepper and remove seeds. Grate
the cheddar cheese coarsely and add the ground meat
along with the raw egg, parsley and salt and pepper
to taste. Stuff and mound the mixture into the pepper
shell. Bake in a 350° oven for 45 minutes in a casserole rubbed lightly with butter; add 1 tablespoon water and seal casserole or small terrine as explained in
Chapter II. Vegetables: seal sauce pans after seasoning to taste; add some butter to bottom of pan to winter squash and no water. If fresh, peel and wrap in
aluminum foil to seal and bake in moderate oven. Add
no water at all to zucchini and just 1 tablespoon to
asparagus spears.

1st Monday Totals:
Calories: *1207*   Carbohydrates: *30*

Supplements: For active non-dieting members of the
family: *Breakfast:* 2 eggs, 1 or 2 slices of wheat toast.
Lunch: rolls or crackers and butter; sherbet. *Dinner.*
oven-browned potatoes; dessert of their choice.

1ST TUESDAY

Breakfast

Menu: *Carbohydrates*

Tomato Juice, ½ cup 5
Dried Chipped Beef, ⅓ cup 0
Cream Cheese, 1 ½ ounces ....1 ½
Coffee or Tea, plain 0

Method:

Smooth out dried chipped beef slices and spread with cream cheese; roll up and secure with tooth picks if necessary. Serve with the tomato juice.

Nutrients and Vitamins:

Protein 23, Calcium 46, Iron 3.1, Vitamin A 2,980,
Thiamine .16, Riboflavin .32, Vitamin C 38,
Niacin 3.2, Fatty Acids 7

Lunch

Menu:
Clam Juice
Pink Salmon Aspic
Sour Cream and Yogurt Topping
Chilled Asparagus
Green Stuffed Olives
Melba Toast
Iced or Hot coffee or Tea

Ingredients: *Carbohydrates*

Clam juice, ½ cup 0
Pink salmon, ⅔ cup 0

Celery, diced, 1 stalk 1

Green onion, diced, with part of tops 1

Green pimiento stuffed olives, sliced, 4 2

Chicken broth, 1 cup 0

Gelatin, unflavored, 1 tablespoon (one envelope) 0

Sour cream and yogurt, 1 tablespoon each 4

Asparagus spears, green, 6 3

Melba toast, rye or wheat, 3 slim pieces 16

Method:

Chill clam juice before serving. Drain salmon, flake or crumble and mix with celery, onion and olives. Place in serving aspic mold. Melt gelatin with the chicken broth and let chill to one-half solid. Add to salmon mixture. Chill until set. Garnish with the parsley sprigs and topping of sour cream and yogurt mixed with garlic salt and lime or lemon juice, to taste. Serve with the melba toast; arrange the asparagus around the aspic or serve separately.

Nutrients and Vitamins:

Protein 40, Calcium 432, Iron 1.14 ½, Vitamin A 270, Thiamine .09, Riboflavin .45, Vitamin C 6, Niacin 12.92, Fatty Acids 13 ½

Dinner

Menu:

Veal Birds en Casserole Parisian
Okra with Tomatoes
Buttered Beets
Coffee, Mint, Lime or Raspberry Sherbet
Small Black Coffee or Espresso

Ingredients: *Carbohydrates*

Veal, thin strips, pounded, boneless, 6 ounces 0
Green onion, sweet pepper, mushrooms, sauce with
chicken broth and arrowroot or cornstarch 17
Okra with tomatoes, okra ½ cup, tomatoes ⅓ cup 9
Beets, ⅓ cup 6
Butter, 1 teaspoon 0
Chicken broth, ½ cup 0

Method:

The butcher will prepare the veal for you if you just
ask. If he does not have time; pound veal till thin and
cut in strips. In the center of each piece place the green
onions, a little chopped pepper, about three mushrooms for each piece of veal. Roll and fasten with
toothpicks. Cook in covered casserole for 45 minutes
in medium oven with the chicken broth. Remove veal
and keep warm in oven. Add enough arrowroot (or
cornstarch) to thicken broth and juices. Season to
taste; serve over the veal.

Nutrients and Vitamins:

Protein 68, Calcium 282, Iron 8.9, Vitamin A 3,300,
Thiamine .31, Riboflavin 1.16, Vitamin C 154,
Niacin 11.39, Fatty Acids 13

1st Tuesday Totals:
Calories: *1103*   Carbohydrates: *65½*

Supplements: For active non-dieting members of the
family: *Breakfast:* more of the same, with buttered
wheat toast or corn meal muffins. *Lunch:* hot bean
soup, Vienna or Italian bread with butter. *Dinner:*
onion soup with croutons; dumplings steamed with
the veal birds, cookies or cake with the sherbet.

1ST WEDNESDAY

Breakfast

Menu:

Canteloupe or Melon Balls
Hot Oatmeal with Half and Half
    topped with
Brown Sugar and Raisins
Buttered Whole Wheat Toast
Coffee or Tea

Ingredients: *Carbohydrates*

Canteloupe, ½ or melon balls, ½ cup 9
Oatmeal, ½ cup 13
Half and half, ½ cup 5
Brown sugar, 1 teaspoon 7
Raisins, dried (soak), 1 tablespoon 4
Whole wheat toast, 1 slice 12
Butter, 1 teaspoon 0

Nutrients and Vitamins:

Protein 16, Calcium 183, Iron .72, Vitamin A 1,230,
Thiamine .12, Riboflavin 4.15,
Vitamin C 19, Niacin 2.01 ½, Fatty Acids 14.7

Lunch

Menu:

Ground Steak a la Scotch Grill
    with
Cheddar Cheese Topping
    on Rye Toast
Sliced Tomatoes
Parsley Sprigs
Coffee or Tea

Ingredients: *Carbohydrates*

Ground round steak or chuck, lean, 6 ounces 0
Egg, raw, 1 0
Cheddar cheese, thick slice to cover toast 0
Rye toast, 1 slice 11
Tomato, ½ large 3

Method:

Mix the ground meat with the egg and seasoned salt,
salt and pepper to taste; whip to mix thoroughly and
to create a light mix (add a little milk if too heavy).
Spread on very lightly toasted rye bread to completely
cover. Place under broiler, 6 inches from heat for
about 6 minutes; withdraw from oven and cover with
cheese. Heat until cheese is melted. Serve garnished
with sliced tomatoes and parsley.

Nutrients and Vitamins:

Protein 14, Calcium 229, Iron .7 ½, Vitamin A
1,230, Thiamine .12, Riboflavin .35 ½,
Vitamin C 19, Niacin 4.15, Fatty Acids 29.8

Dinner

Menu:

Braised or Broiled Lamb Chops
Pineapple Russe
Broccoli with Sour Cream Topping
Spinach
Coffee or Tea

Ingredients: *Carbohydrates*

Lamb chops, no fat, with bones, 6 to 8 ounces 0

Pineapple, 1 large slice, fresh or canned, drained 6

Broccoli, fresh or frozen, ½ cup 4

Sour cream topping, 1 tablespoon 1

Spinach, fresh or frozen, ½ cup 3

Method:

Season lamb chops to taste and braise in pan with a scant amount of oil, or just salt. Add pineapple to pan juices and braise on both sides. Cook broccoli and spinach with masking tape (see Chapter II). Stir lime or lemon juice and garlic salt into the sour cream, to taste. Serve over broccoli.

Nutrients and Vitamins:

Protein 42 ½, Calcium 152, Iron 3.18, Vitamin A 2,770, Thiamine .42, Riboflavin .54, Vitamin C 132, Niacin .57, Fatty Acids 41

1st Wednesday Totals:
Calories: *1096*   Carbohydrates: *78*

Supplements: For active non-dieting members of the family: *Breakfast:* simply larger servings if desired. *Lunch:* bean soup, French fried potatoes. *Dinner:* clams with sauce; or mussels; or snails; fruit with cheese; or ice cream for dessert.

Note:

These first three days of menus are rather spartan: designed to clear the system and get the dieter off to a good start. As the days progress, more and more comforting and delicious food is given, but still within the framework of the ideal: about 1200 to 1400 calories per day for a gradual weight loss of around two to three pounds per week. Every day's nutrient and vitamin requirements are met. If, every ten days or so, a wild desire for a piece of candy or cake comes about, do eat it. It will set you back about a half-pound that week, but who knows? Your system might need it. Or, if you feel hungry in the middle of the night or at any time during a frustrating day, please drink a glass of low-fat milk; the calories are negligible and the benefits great.

IST THURSDAY

Breakfast

Menu: *Carbohydrates*

Vegetable-tomato juice, ½ cup 5
Soft-boiled or poached egg, 1 0
Whole wheat toast, ½ slice 6
Butter, 1 teaspoon 0
Coffee or tea with lemon 0

Nutrients and Vitamins:

Protein 9, Calcium 72 ½, Iron 2.1 ½, Vitamin A 730, Thiamine .8, Riboflavin .2, Vitamin C 63, Niacin .1 ½, Fatty Acids 11

Lunch

Menu:

Ham and Asparagus Supreme
    with
Cheddar Cheese Sauce
    on Toast Points
Iced Coffee with Vanilla Ice Cream

Ingredients: *Carbohydrates*

Whole wheat bread, ½ slice 6
Ham, 1 medium slice, precooked 0
Green asparagus, 6 spears, drained 3
Cheddar cheese sauce 3
Vanilla ice cream, 1 tablespoon ....3 ½

Method:

Toast bread and cut into three sections and place on
plate. Cover with ham and arrange asparagus spears
on top. To make cheese sauce, mix ⅓ cup dry nonfat
milk with ½ cup chicken broth (see Additional Recipes) and ¼ cup sharp Cheddar cheese. Thicken with
arrowroot to gravy consistency. Heat and stir until
smooth. Serve ice coffee topped with the ice cream.

Nutrients and Vitamins:

Protein 33.7, Calcium 64 ½, Iron 5.8 ½, Vitamin A
1420, Thiamine .55, Riboflavin .58 ½, Vitamin C 17,
Niacin 4.7 ½, Fatty Acids 29 ½

35

Dinner

Menu:

> Pork Chops Provencale
>> with
>
> Applesauce and Wine
> String Beans with Mushrooms
> Baked Carrots with Tarragon
> Tossed Green Salad
>> with
>
> Cottage Cheese Dressing

Ingredients: *Carbohydrates*

Pork chops, 2, lean, 3 ½ ounces each with bone 0
Applesauce, unsweetened, ⅓ cup
   and white wine, ¼ cup ....8 ½
String beans, ½ cup with ⅓ cup mushrooms 6
Baked carrots, ½ cup ....4 ½
Romaine lettuce, ¼ head 2
Cottage cheese salad dressing 7

Method:

Sprinkle frying pan with salt and pepper; add chops and braise lightly and slowly on both sides. Spread applesauce over them after transferring the chops to an oven-type dish with lid. Add wine and seal the lid with tape; cook on lowest heat for about 45 minutes or until tender. Cook string beans using tape method. The carrots should be put into the oven along with the chops; for method see Additional Recipes. Cottage cheese dressing for the lettuce may also be found in

Additional Recipes. In the summer lobster tails or lamb chops may be substituted for pork chops.

Nutrients and Vitamins:

Protein 50½, Calcium 195, Iron 8.9½, Vitamin A 10,920, Thiamine .144, Riboflavin .49½, Niacin 11.38, Vitamin C 35, Fatty Acids 35

1st Thursday Totals:
Calories *1,458*   Carbohydrates *54½*

Supplements: For active non-dieting members of the family: *Lunch:* fruit compote or salad and full slice of toast. *Dinner:* oven-baked potatoes; vanilla ice cream with chocolate sauce for dessert.

IST FRIDAY

Breakfast

Menu: *Carbohydrates*

Banana, sliced, ½ of large, ⅓ cup milk 15
Scrambled eggs with yogurt, 2 tablespoons 2
Bacon, crisp, 2 slices 0
Coffee or tea, plain 0

Method:

Sweeten banana slightly if desired. Use low fat milk or plain yogurt for topping. Whip eggs and stir in plain yogurt; add salt and pepper to taste. Fry bacon slowly until just crisp; keep warm in paper towel in low oven. Drain bacon fat from pan, leaving just enough for the scrambled eggs. Add ⅛ cup dry milk to low fat milk, for needed calcium.

Nutrients and Vitamins:

Protein 24, Calcium 380, Iron 3.2 ½, Vitamin A 1,290, Thiamine 5.39 ½, Riboflavin 1.47 ½, Vitamin C 7 ½, Niacin 1.21 ½, Fatty Acids 22

Lunch

Menu:

Tomato Juice
Herbed Steamed Chicken
Fresh Celery
Grilled Cottage Cheese Patty Melt
Jumbo Green Olives

Ingredients: Carbohydrates

Tomato juice, 1 cup 10
Steamed chicken, 6 ounces, boned 0
Celery, 2 stalks 2
Whole wheat toast, ½ slice 6
Cottage cheese, 4 ounces, slim-type 2
Green bell pepper or green chili pepper 0
Jumbo green olives, up to seven 1

Method:

See Additional Recipes for Herbed Steamed Chicken. Clean and dethread the celery and cut in three-inch pieces. Toast the bread lightly on one side only. Mix the cottage cheese with finely minced green pepper, salt, seasoned salt and pepper; mound on the un-toasted side of the bread and grill under the broiler for about three minutes or until bread edges are crusty. Serve the chicken cold or hot along with the celery, salted if desired, the patty melt and the olives.

Nutrients and Vitamins:

Protein 54, Calcium 168 ½, Iron 4.5 ½
Vitamin A 560, Thiamine .21, Riboflavin .52 ½,
Vitamin C 16, Niacin 20.15 ½, Fatty acids 13.3 ½

Dinner

Menu:

Filet of Sole with Champagne Sauce
French Cut String Beans with Crumbled Bacon
Crookneck Yellow Squash with Chicken Broth
Gruyère Swiss Cheese and Fresh Apple
Coffee or Espresso

Ingredients:	*Carbohydrates*
Filet of sole, 6 ounces	0
White dry wine, ⅓ cup	1
Parsley butter, 1 teaspoon	0
String beans, ½ cup	3
Bacon, 1 strip, cooked crisp	0
Crookneck squash, 1 cup	8
Swiss cheese, gruyère, 2 wedges (1 ½ ounces)	1
Apple, fresh, ½	9

Method:

In an oven baking dish place the fish; pour the wine over it and dot with butter mixed with finely minced parsley. Bake in 400° oven until just white (do not overcook, because it will fall apart). Garnish with lemon or lime slices. Cook string beans according to tape method. Fry bacon until quite crisp but not burned; set aside and crumble over string beans at serving time. See Additional Recipes for the squash recipe. Serve cheese with apple wedges for dessert.

Nutrients and Vitamins:

Protein 57, Calcium 529, Iron 12.83, Vitamin A 1,640, Thiamine .21 ½, Riboflavin .91 ½, Vitamin C 24.9 ½, Niacin 4.12 ½, Fatty Acids 19 ½

1st Friday Totals:
Calories *1,269*   Carbohydrates *60*

Supplements: For active non-dieting members of the family: *Breakfast:* more juice, toast, butter and even jelly, if desired. *Lunch:* a whole slice of patty melt; enough chicken to satisfy (not more than 8 ounces). Dessert if quite active. *Dinner:* hash-brown or oven-browned potatoes; Vienna rolls and butter.

IST SATURDAY

Breakfast

Menu:

Tomato Juice
Pork Sausages
Buckwheat Pancake
    with
Poached Egg
Coffee or tea

Ingredients: *Carbohydrates*

Tomato juice, ½ cup 5
Link sausages, 2 fried 0
Buckwheat pancake, use pancake mix 6
Yogurt, plain, 2 tablespoons ....1 ½
Nonfat dry milk, 2 tablespoons ....2 ½
Baking soda, ¼ teaspoon 0
Poached egg, 1 0

Method:

Fry sausages until golden crisp; drain and keep warm in oven. Mix enough pancake batter for one, or many more if cooking for the family. But if just one the ration should be: about ⅓ cup pancake mix; the liquid to be comprised of 2 tablespoons yogurt, 2 tablespoons nonfat dry milk, and enough water to make a heavy cream. Stir into pancake mix until batter seems just right. Fry in pan after the link sausages have been removed or on pancake grill. Place poached egg on top of pancake and serve with the sausages and tomato juice.

Nutrients and Vitamins:

Protein, 21, Calcium 229 ½, Iron 3.7 ½,
Vitamin A 1,837, Thiamine .18 ½, Riboflavin .45,
Vitamin C 39 ½, Niacin 12.0, Fatty Acids 23

Lunch

Menu:

Tuna Stuffed Tomato
Cottage Cheese
Green Olives and Celery Strips
Coffee or Tea

Ingredients:	*Carbohydrates*
Tomato, 1 medium	6
Tuna, 3 ounces, water pack	0
Celery, 1 stalk	1
Yogurt, plain, 4 tablespoons	2½
Dillweed, about 1 teaspoon	0
Cottage cheese, 4 ounces (½ cup)	2
Green olives, jumbo, 3 to 4	½

Method:

Slice off top of tomato and hollow it out a little. Drain and flake the tuna; mix the yogurt and dillweed in thoroughly. Use a little more yogurt if needed for moistness. Mound the mixture on the tomato. Clean and dethread the celery and cut into strips; serve along with the cottage cheese (seasoned to taste), olives and the stuffed tomato.

Nutrients and Vitamins:

Protein 40½, Calcium 193, Iron 3.01 ½,
Vitamin A 1,835, Thiamine .17, Riboflavin .43,
Vitamin C 38, Niacin 11.0, Fatty Acids 11 ½

Dinner

Menu:

Steak Châteaubriand
Carrots Julienne
Petite Onions
Brussels Sprouts
Sherbet
Coffee or Espresso

Ingredients: *Carbohydrates*

Steak, filet mignon, about 2-inches thick 0
                    (6 ounces)
Carrots, strips, 2 medium 10
Small white onions, about 5 9
Brussels sprouts, ½ cup 6
Sherbet, ½ cup 21
Brandy, ½ cup; wine, Burgundy, ⅓ cup, to
    be used for steak 0

Method:

Trim all fat from steak; sprinkle liberally with seasoned coarse ground pepper and braise in heavy pan
(with lid) that goes into the oven. Sprinkle salt in the
bottom of the pan and braise the steak quite slowly
until seared on both sides. Add the carrots and onions
and pour the brandy and wine over all. Seal the lid on
very thoroughly with masking tape so that no steam
is allowed to escape. Place in pre-heated 250° oven
and bake for about one hour or until quite tender. To
serve: slice the steak into diagonal slices if desired.
Cook brussels sprouts using tape or foil.

Nutrients and Vitamins:

Protein 48 ½, Calcium 305 ½, Iron 6.4, Vitamin A
12,530, Thiamine .25, Riboflavin .63,
Vitamin C 45, Niacin 7.6, Fatty Acids 24

1st Saturday Totals:
   Calories: *1602*   Carbohydrates: *73*

Supplements: For active non-dieting members of the family: *Breakfast:* two additional pancakes and another sausage. Syrup or jam, if desired. *Lunch:* a slice of pineapple in lettuce cup for a cottage cheese salad. Bread or rolls with butter. *Dinner:* duchesse potatoes, a dinner roll with butter, and cookies or cake with the sherbet.

IST SUNDAY

Breakfast

Menu:

Thick Broiled Tomato Slices
  with
Parmesan Cheese
Chicken Livers Sauté
Scrambled Egg
Coffee or Tea

Ingredients: Carbohydrates

Fresh tomato, large 6
Parmesan cheese, 1 ounce 2
Chicken livers, about 4, cut up 6
Arrowroot, 1 to 2 teaspoons 2
Egg, large fresh 0
Yogurt, plain, 2 tablespoons ....1 ½

Method:

Thinly slice off top and bottom of tomato and cut the remainder into two thick slices. Salt and pepper to taste and sprinkle Parmesan cheese thickly over each slice. Broil for about four minutes after preparing the following chicken livers: clean, remove any fat, cut in two or three pieces; drain and blot dry and then add enough arrowroot to flour completely. Season with pepper; sprinkle pan with salt, braise and turn to sear both sides on low heat, then add enough dry white wine to keep chicken livers moist until done. Whip egg and add yogurt and seasoning to taste. Cook in pan or skillet with "Pam" if possible (a vegetable sealer) or a little butter.

Nutrients and Vitamins:

Protein 22, Calcium 252, Iron 5.17, Vitamin A 32,881, Thiamine .32 ½, Riboflavin 2.69 ½, Vitamin C 54, Niacin 8.15, Fatty Acids 17 ½

Lunch

Menu:

Grilled Cheese and Bacon
   on Toast
Tossed Lettuce Salad
   with
Hungarian Dressing
Coffee or Tea

Ingredients:	*Carbohydrates*
Toast, white, enriched	12
Sharp Cheddar cheese, 3 slices, thin	0
Bacon, 2 slices, halved	0
Lettuce, ¼ small head	3
Yogurt, plain, 2 tablespoons	1 ½
Cottage cheese, slim-type, ⅓ cup	2
Paprika and seasoning	0

Method:

Toast bread slice on side only; blanch bacon; arrange slices of cheddar cheese on untoasted side of bread. Place bacon on top and broil until bacon is crispy and cheese somewhat melted. On cleaned and drained ¼ head of lettuce pour the following dressing: in blender or by hand, beat yogurt, cottage cheese, paprika and seasoning of your choice, such as green onion tops and/or chives, and salt and pepper. A small glass of Burgundy might be had with this lunch.

Nutrients and Vitamins:

Protein 26, Calcium 356, Iron 1.40 ½,
Vitamin A 1021, Thiamine .64 ½, Ribboflavin .56 ½,
Vitamin C 9, Niacin .61, Fatty Acids 19 ½

Dinner

Menu:

Melon Compote
Steamed Chicken, Chicken Velouté Sauce
    with
Spinach Soufflé Dressing
Cinnamon Apple Ring
Coleslaw with Caraway
Small Black Coffee

Ingredients: *Carbohydrates*

Melon balls (frozen) 9
Chicken, 6 ounces, without skin 0
Spinach soufflé dressing, ½ cup serving 9
Velouté sauce, ⅓ cup 2
Cinnamon apple ring, 1 18
Cabbage, raw, ½ cup 2
Coleslaw Dressing, ¼ cup ....2 ½

Method:

Place all the giblets and neck from a chicken in the bottom of a heavy kettle large enough for the bird; add, cut in pieces, a large carrot, two or three stalks celery, one large onion. Then add two bay leaves and two or three pinches of rosemary and thyme. Twelve peppercorns and salt to taste should then be added. Place (or float) an inverted pie tin, after adding about five cups of water to the ingredients, on top, and put the chicken on its side on the tin. Seal on lid with tape and cook slowly for about three hours, or until tender. See Additional Recipes for Spinach Soufflé Dressing, Caraway Seed Coleslaw Dressing and Velouté Sauce. The apple rings may be purchased, already prepared, in a jar in the markets.

Nutrients and Vitamins:

Protein 52, Calcium 294, Iron 7.9 ½, Vitamin A 18,060, Thiamine .41, Riboflavin .83, Vitamin C 71 ½, Niacin 22.26 ½, Fatty Acids 18 ½

1st Sunday Totals:
Calories: *1,211*   Carbohydrates: *78 ½*

Supplements: For active non-dieting members of the family: *Breakfast:* mild green chili peppers; toast, biscuits, or muffins with jam. *Lunch:* tomato slices with herbed Italian dressing. *Dinner:* angel food cake with strawberry filling with whip cream. (Small sweet bliss potatoes, peeled and left whole, may be steamed along with the chicken, if desired.)

2ND MONDAY

Breakfast

Menu:

Tomato juice, ½ cup 5
Dried chip beef, ⅓ cup 0
Cream cheese, 1 ½ ounces ....1 ½
Coffee or tea, plain 0

Method:

See 1st Tuesday breakfast

Nutrients and Vitamins:

Protein 23, Calcium 46, Iron 3.10, Vitamin A 2,980, Thiamine .16, Riboflavin .32, Vitamin C 38, Niacin 3.2, Fatty Acids 12

Lunch

Menu:

Lobster Salad
Green Asparagus Spears
Coffee or Tea

Ingredients: *Carbohydrates*

Boiled or steamed lobster, 6 ounces 0
Dressing for marinade 0
Lettuce, 4 leaves 1
Hard-boiled egg, 1 0
Capers, 1 teaspoon 0
Mayonnaise, 1 tablespoon 0
Asparagus spears, 6 3

Method:

Cut cold lobster meat into small chunks. Marinate in Italian-style dressing. Drain thoroughly after two or three hours; place on shredded lettuce and garnish with olives, hard-boiled egg slices or wedges. Top with mayonnaise and capers. Place asparagus in clumps of two or three around the salad on serving plate.

Nutrients and Vitamins:

Protein 38, Calcium 184, Iron 4.26,
Vitamin A 1,840, Thiamine .21, Riboflavin .37,
Vitamin C 21, Niacin 4.12, Fatty Acids 29

Dinner

Menu:

Steamed Knockwurst
   with Cabbage
Chive Cottage Cheese Salad
   with Tomato Slices
Sherbet
Rye Bread and Butter
Coffee or Tea

Ingredients: **Carbohydrates**

Knockwurst, 1 (kosher-style) 1
Cabbage, ⅓ medium head 9
Condiments: chili sauce, mustard 4
Chive cottage cheese, 3 ounces, slim-type 3
Tomato, 1 medium 6
Rye bread, 1 slice, ½-inch thick 12
Butter, 1 teaspoon 0
Sherbet, ½ cup ....27 ½

Method:

Cook cabbage in a fairly heavy kettle, with lid; use only about ⅓ cup water. Place knockwurst on top. Seal lid and cook very slowly for about 35 minutes. Test, and reseal, if necessary. Garnish salad with parsley. Serve condiments with the meal.

Nutriments and Vitamins:

Protein 28 ½, Calcium 256 ½, Iron 6.8,
Vitamin A 2,340, Thiamine .63, Riboflavin 1.69,
Vitamin C 55, Niacin 7.8 ½, Fatty Acids 19

2nd Monday Totals
Calories: *1,154*   Carbohydrates: *73*

Supplements: For non-dieting members of the family: *Breakfast:* scrambled eggs with a little yogurt. *Lunch:* a roll or bread with butter should be sufficient. *Dinner:* buttered parsleyed potatoes; cookies or cake with sherbet.

Note: Please drink a glass of mixed non-fat dried milk and low-fat milk with lunch, dinner or at bedtime, because the calcium level is not adequate for this day.

2ND TUESDAY

Breakfast

Menu: *Carbohydrates*

Grapefruit Juice, ½ cup sweetened 16
Fried Ham, 3 ounces (use Pam instead of fat) 0
Poached Egg, 1 0
Whole Wheat Toast, ½ slice 6
Coffee or Tea 0

Nutrients and Vitamins:

Protein 28, Calcium 68 ½, Iron 4.8 ½,
Vitamin A 840, Thiamine .61, Riboflavin .39 ½,
Vitamin C 78, Niacin 4.2 ½, Fatty Acids 26.4 ½

Lunch

Menu:

Sliced Tongue
 with
Cream of Horseradish Sauce
Spinach with Minced Egg
Hot or Cold Coffee with Ice Cream Topping

Ingredients: *Carbohydrates*

Sliced tongue, 3 ounces, hot or cold 0
Cream of horseradish sauce, 4 tablespoons .... 2 ½
Spinach, ½ cup 3
Hard-boiled egg, 1, minced or grated 0
Ice cream, 1 tablespoon 3

51

Method:

Three ounces of tongue is about 4 center slices. For horseradish sauce see Additional Recipes. Cook spinach using foil or tape method. Sprinkle the grated egg over the spinach before serving. Top iced or hot coffee with ice cream.

Nutrients and Vitamins:

Protein 28, Calcium 218, Iron 3.8 ½, Vitamin A 10,841, Thiamine .17 ½, Riboflavin .66 ½, Vitamin C 28, Niacin 3.58, Fatty Acids 25

Dinner

Menu:

Breast of Chicken
  with
Soy Sauce Marinade
Green French Cut String Beans
Sliced Cucumbers
  with
Dilled Dressing
Fruit with Swiss Cheese
Coffee or Tea or Espresso

Ingredients: *Carbohydrates*

Chicken breast, 6 ounces 0
Green beans, ⅔ cup 3
Cucumber, ½ of large 1
Dressing, 3 tablespoons .... 1 ½
Pear, apple, peach or other fruit, ½ 16
Gruyère swiss cheese, 1 ounce 1

Method:

Chicken and cucumber recipes may be found in Additional Recipes.

Nutrients and Vitamins:

Protein 50, Calcium 364 ½, Iron 4.4,
Vitamin A 1,016, Thiamine .26, Riboflavin .52 ½,
Vitamin C 17 ½, Niacin 20.9, Fatty Acids 15 ½

2nd Tuesday Totals:
Calories: *1,352*   Carbohydrates: *53*

Supplements: For active non-dieting members of the family: *Breakfast:* additional toast, jelly and another egg, if desired. *Lunch:* bean soup or clam chowder; ice cream. *Dinner:* rice pilaff or pork fried rice; dinner rolls and butter.

Note: Here also, the calcium level is not reached: please drink a glass of mixed non-fat dried milk and low fat milk sometime during the day.

2ND WEDNESDAY

Breakfast

Menu: *Carbohydrates*

Orange Juice, ½ cup .... 13 ½
Buckwheat Pancake, 1 (six-inch diameter) 6
Butter, 1 teaspoon 0
Poached or Soft-Boiled Egg, 1 0
Coffee or Tea 0

Method:

Mix pancake batter according to directions on package, except use yogurt, mixed non-fat dried milk with skim milk, and a little baking soda. Place egg on top of pancake, if desired, and serve with the orange juice and coffee.

Nutrients and Vitamins:

Protein 10, Calcium 186 ½, Iron 2.4 ½,
Vitamin A 1121, Thiamine .21, Riboflavin .26,
Vitamin C 57, Niacin .61, Fatty Acids 13 ½

Lunch

Menu:

Broiled Baked Ham and Swiss Cheese
   on Rye or Wheat Toast
String Bean and Onion Salad
   with
Vinagrette Dressing
Milk

Ingredients: *Carbohydrates*

Ham, 1 three-ounce slice, without bone   0
Natural Swiss cheese, 1 one-ounce slice ....   ½
Rye or whole wheat bread, 1 slice 12
String beans, ½ cup   3
Onion, red, ¼ medium size .... 4 ½
Sugar, 1 teaspoon   6
Milk, low-fat, 1 cup 13

Method:

Toast one side of bread lightly; place the ham and cheese on the untoasted side. Broil until bread

edges are crusty and cheese melted somewhat. See
Additional Recipes for the string bean and onion
salad. The glass of milk is important; if you do not
like the flavor as is, add some double-strength coffee
to it.

Nutrients and Vitamins:

Protein 39 ½, Calcium 639 ½, Iron 3.8,
Vitamin A, 1220, Thiamine .66 ½, Riboflavin 1.31,
Vitamin C 13 ½, Niacin 3.21 ½, Fatty Acids 50

Dinner

Menu:

Sautéed Chicken Livers
Rice Pilaff
Broccoli Amandine
Herbed Tomatoes
Coffee or Tea

Ingredients: *Carbohydrates*

Chicken livers, 4 ounces 12
Arrowroot, 2 teaspoons 6
Butter, 1 teaspoon 6
Rice, converted, ½ cup .... 22 ½
Chicken broth, ½ cup 0
Broccoli, 1 cup 8
Slivered almonds, 1 teaspoon 1
Tomato, 1 medium, or 5 slices canned baby 6
Oil, 1 teaspoon 0
Vinegar, 1 teaspoon 0
Parsley, 1 tablespoon; thyme, a pinch, rosemary,
    a pinch 0

Method:

Dust chicken livers thoroughly with arrowroot; melt butter very slowly to cover bottom of skillet. Add livers and turn up heat, turning often until done. Cook converted rice according to package suggestions, but do add ½ cup chicken broth for every ½ cup rice. Cook broccoli according to tape or foil method. Serve topped with slivered almonds. Slice tomato and marinate for a short time in oil, vinegar and herbs. Salt and pepper to taste. Serve in salad bowl.

Nutrients and Vitamins:

Protein 38, Calcium 252, Iron 13.0 ½,
Vitamin A 67,400, Thiamine .55, Riboflavin 4.80,
Vitamin C 182, Niacin 19.8, Fatty Acids 16

2nd Wednesday Totals:
Calories: *1169½*   Carbohydrates: *114*

Supplements: For active non-dieting members of the family: *Breakfast*: up to one cup orange juice, two or more pancakes (more for a 17- to 20-year-old boy or very hard-working man); For the latter, perhaps two eggs. For both, syrup on pancakes, if desired, and more butter. *Lunch*: cream of chicken soup; for dessert, melon, or other light fare.

2ND THURSDAY

Breakfast

Menu:

Tomato Juice
Scrambled Eggs with Swiss Cheese
on
Toast Points
Coffee or Tea

Ingredients: *Carbohydrates*

Tomato juice, ½ cup 5
Eggs, 2 0
Yogurt, plain, 2 tablespoons .... 1 ½
Butter, 1 teaspoon 0
Swiss cheese, natural, 1 ounce 1
Rye bread, 1 slice, lightly toasted 12

Method:

Heat butter slowly in skillet; whip eggs with yogurt
and add minced or grated Swiss cheese. Scramble the
eggs and serve on rye toast points, or on full slice, as
desired. Serve with the tomato juice.

Nutrients and Vitamins:

Protein 24, Calcium 395, Iron 3.8 ½,
Vitamin A 3,391, Thiamine .24, Riboflavin .49 ½,
Vitamin C 36, Niacin 1.11, Fatty Acids 25 ½

Lunch

Menu:

>Stuffed Avocado
> with
>Shrimp Salad
>Carrot Sticks
>Jumbo Green Olives
>Coffee or Tea

Ingredients: *Carbohydrates*

Avocado (California variety), ½, five ounces	6
Shrimp, 3 ounces, canned (broken)	0
Celery, 1 stalk	1
Mayonnaise, 1 tablespoon	0
Yogurt, plain, 2 tablespoons	1½
Carrot sticks, 6 slender (½ small carrot)	2½
Green olives, jumbo size, 7	1

Method:

Halve the avocado and leave as is with peel or peel, as desired. Mound the drained shrimp, de-threaded chopped celery, mayonnaise mixture in the avocado. Serve with the carrot sticks and olives.

Nutrients and Vitamins:

Protein 28½, Calcium 226, Iron 4.6½,
Vitamin A 3,591, Thiamine .17½, Riboflavin .31,
Vitamin C 20½, Niacin 3.91½, Fatty Acids 38½

Dinner

Menu:

Pork Chops
  with
Steamed Caraway Sauerkraut
Onion Rings
Parsleyed Steamed Potatoes
Sweet Yellow Corn on the Cob
Espresso

Ingredients: *Carbohydrates*

Pork chop, large shoulder cut, 1, lean 0
Sauerkraut, 1 cup, drained 7
Onion, ½ medium .... 5 ½
Potato, 1 red bliss, peeled, medium size 20
Yellow corn, 1 ear, medium size 16
Butter, for corn, 1 teaspoon 0

Method:

See Additional Recipes for pork chop and sauerkraut recipe.

Nutrients and Vitamins:

Protein 23, Calcium 91 ½, Iron, 4.4,
Vitamin A 390, Thiamine .87, Riboflavin .41,
Vitamin C 55, Niacin 6.4, Fatty Acids 26

2nd Thursday Totals:
  Calories: *1,475*   Carbohydrates: *81*

Supplements: For active non-dieting members of the family: *Breakfast:* more tomato juice and another slice of toast, if desired. *Lunch:* rolls with butter or margarine; ice cream or fruit pie. *Dinner:* clam chowder, ½ cup; rye bread and butter; fruit and cheese for dessert.

2ND FRIDAY

Breakfast

Menu: *Carbohydrates*

Orange Juice, ½ Cup (frozen) ....13 ½
Corn Flakes, Medium-Sized Bowl 24
    with
Raspberries, ¼ Cup (frozen) 14
Milk, low-fat, ½ Cup .... 6 ½
Coffee or Tea 0

Nutrients and Vitamins:

Protein 7 ½, Calcium 180, Iron .14 ½,
Vitamin A 794, Thiamine .28, Riboflavin .29,
Vitamin C 66, Niacin .13, Fatty Acids, 4

Lunch

Menu:

Broiled Herbed Ground Beef
    with
Onion Rings and Piquant Sauce
    on Rye Toast
Pineapple with Cottage Cheese
Coffee or Tea

Ingredients;   *Carbohydrates*

Ground round steak, 3 ounces 0
Nonfat dry milk, ¼ cup 10½
Water, 2 tablespoons 0
Parsley, 3 or 4 sprigs, snipped 0
Chili sauce, 1 tablespoon 4
Onion, ½ medium (use center slices) 9
Rye bread, 1 slice 12
Pineapple, 1 small slice (canned) 13
Cottage cheese, ⅓ cup, slim-type 3

Method:

See Additional Recipes for Broiled Herbed Ground
Beef on toast with onion rings and also for
Piquant Sauce. Season cottage cheese to taste.

Nutrients and Vitamins:

Protein 48 ½, Calcium 302 ½, Iron 4.5,
Vitamin A 425, Thiamine .84, Riboflavin 1.20,
Vitamin C 15, Niacin 6.20, Fatty Acids 10

Dinner

Menu:

Shrimp Cocktail
  with
Piquant Sauce
Jellied Madrilene
Scallops Nicole in Wine Sauce
Baked Winter Squash
French Fried Potatoes
Coffee, Espresso or Tea

Ingredients:	*Carbohydrates*
Shrimp, 3 ounces	0
Piquant sauce	4
Jellied madrilene, ½ cup	10
Scallops, 6 or 7	0
Wine sauce	3
Baked winter squash, ½ cup	11 ½
French fried potatoes, 10 pieces, frozen-type	15

Method:

Mix or top shrimp cocktail with piquant sauce (see Additional Recipes). Add a little chopped celery to cocktail, if desired; the calories will be negligible. Buy canned Madrilene it will spare untold cooking and be just as good. See Additional Recipes for Scallops Nicole. Bake winter squash (frozen) using tape method. Fresh squash should be peeled, seasoned and wrapped in aluminum foil with sealed edges and baked at 400° for 45 minutes to 1 hour or until tender. Heat French fried potatoes according to package directions.

Nutrients and Vitamins:

Protein 60, Calcium 262 ½, Iron 9.7,
Vitamin A 8,430, Thiamine .32, Riboflavin .40 ½,
Vitamin C 38, Niacin 7.53, Fatty Acids 38

2nd Friday Totals:
Calories *1,341* Carbohydrates *153*

Supplements: For active non-dieting members of the family: since carbohydrates are high in this menu, they should simply take a little larger helping of everything on the menu. But it is important that they have a glass of milk for lunch and could have a light dessert with dinner.

2ND SATURDAY

Breakfast

Menu:

Cantaloupe or Melon Balls
Hot Oatmeal
Brown Sugar and Raisins
Buttered Whole Wheat Toast
Coffee or Tea

Ingredients: *Carbohydrates*

Cantaloupe, ½ or melon balls, ½ cup 9
Oatmeal, ½ cup 13
Half and half, ⅓ cup 5
Brown sugar, 1 teaspoon 7
Raisins, dried (soak), 1 tablespoon 4
Whole wheat toast, 1 slice 12
Butter, 1 teaspoon 0

Nutrients and Vitamins:

Protein 16, Calcium 183, Iron .72, Vitamin A 1,230,
Thiamine .2, Riboflavin 4.15, Vitamin C 19,
Niacin 2.01 ½, Fatty Acids 14.7

Lunch

Menu:

Tomato Juice
Ham and Asparagus
    with
Swiss Cheese Sauce
on Toast Points
Iced or Hot Coffee with Vanilla Ice Cream

Ingredients: *Carbohydrates*

Tomato juice, ½ cup 5
Ham 1 medium slice, precooked 0
Green asparagus, 6 spears 3
Swiss cheese sauce 3
Whole wheat toast, ½ slice 6
Vanilla ice cream, 1 tablespoon .... 3 ½

Method:

For ham and asparagus, follow recipe of lst Thursday. Serve the coffee topped with the ice cream.

Nutrients and Vitamins:

Protein 35.7, Calcium 80, Iron 6.7 ½,
Vitamin A 3,060, Thiamine .63, Riboflavin .64 ½,
Vitamin C 52, Niacin 5.5 ½, Fatty Acids 29.5 ½

Dinner

Menu:

Beef Consommé
Filet Mignon (or other lean steak)
Mushrooms
Italian Green Beans
Baked Potato
    with
Chived Cream Topping
Coffee or Tea

Ingredients: *Carbohydrates*

Beef consommé, 1 cup 0
Steak, 4 ounces, no fat 0
Mushrooms, 7 medium or ⅓ cup canned 3
Italian string beans, ½ cup 3
Baked potato, ½ ....10 ½
Chive-cream topping, 3 tablespoons ....1 ½

Method:

Season steak to taste and broil or pan fry in a little salt, very slowly for tenderness. Cook beans using tape method. Serve the baked potato with the Chived Cream Topping (See Additional Recipes).

Nutrients and Vitamins:

Protein 27 ½, Calcium 78, Iron 4.36, Vitamin A 436, Thiamine .64, Riboflavin .49 ½, Vitamin C 20, Niacin 6.11, Fatty Acids 5 ½

2nd Saturday Totals:
Calories *1,304*   Carbohydrates *88 ½*

Supplements: For active non-dieting members of the family: *Breakfast:* simply larger servings if desired. *Lunch:* more bread and larger servings, particularly more cheese. Ice cream and cookies for dessert, or dessert of their choice if it contains milk.

2ND SUNDAY

Breakfast

Menu:

Apple Juice
Pork Sausages
Buckwheat Pancakes
Poached Egg
Coffee or Tea

Ingredients:	*Carbohydrates*
Apple juice, frozen, diluted, ½ cup	11
Link sausages, 3	0
Buckwheat pancake, 1	6
Yogurt, plain, 2 tablespoons	1½
Nonfat dried milk, 2 tablespoons	2½
Poached egg, 1	0

Method:

Frozen apple juice is a fairly new product and has no sugar added, but is enriched with Vitamin C. For the rest of the method see last Saturday breakfast.

Nutrients and Vitamins:

Protein 40½, Calcium 186, Iron 2.8½,
Vitamin A 242, Thiamine .12½, Riboflavin .42,
Vitamin C 29, Niacin 11.0, Fatty Acids 11½

Lunch

Menu:

Pink Salmon
   with
Dill Sauce and Capers
Celery and Green Olives
Cottage Cheese and Tomato Salad
Milk

Ingredients: *Carbohydrates*

Salmon, pink, 3 ounces 0
Dillweed, 1 teaspoon 0
Yogurt, 4 tablespoons 2½
Capers, drained, 1 teaspoon 0
Celery, 1 eight-inch stalk 1
Cottage cheese, ½ cup 2
Tomato, 1 medium 6
Milk, low fat, 1 cup 13

Method:

Drain salmon and mix with dill, yogurt and capers.
It is as delightful as a sudden breeze on a hot day! Cut
celery in diagonal 2-inch pieces. If tomatoes are cost-
ly, buy the canned baby sliced firm ones. Serve about
5 to 6 slices.

Nutrients and Vitamins:

Protein 40½, Calcium 497, Iron 3.01 ½,
Vitamin A 1,837, Thiamine .18 ½, Riboflavin .45,
Vitamin C 45, Niacin 12.0, Fatty Acids 11

Dinner

Menu:

Baked Ham
 with
Apricot Sauce
Baked Yams
Lima Beans
Sliced Beets with Onion Rings
Small Black Coffee

Ingredients:	*Carbohydrates*
Baked ham, 3 ounces, without bone	0
Apricot nectar, ½ cup	15
Dark brown sugar, 1 tablespoon	13
Sherry wine, ¼ cup	0
Arrowroot, 1 teaspoon	1
Pinch of cinnamon and cloves	0
Deep yellow baked yam or sweet potato, ½	17 ½
Sliced beets, ⅓ cup	8
Lima beans, ½ cup	24
Onion, ⅓ medium, red	3 ½
Vinegar, wine, garlic flavored	0
Oil, 1 teaspoon	0

Method:

Remove all fat and gelatin from baked ham. Make
enough sauce (half again) to cover ham. Heat or bake
in a 350° oven and baste occasionally. Bake the yam
or yams at the same time (they will need to be started
earlier, unless you are baking a 5-pound ham, which
takes two hours). Mix the apricot nectar, brown
sugar, sherry wine, cinnamon and cloves together in
sauce pan and bring to a boil; thicken with arrowroot

or cornstarch. Serve in sauce boat to garnish ham. Cook lima beans according to tape method. Drain beets and add very finely sliced onion pieces or rings, then add oil and vinegar. Season to taste. Should be served in a salad bowl for best enjoyment and full nutrient intake. There should be no desire for a dessert, since the sweet sour combination leaves one completely satisfied.

Nutrients and Vitamins:

Protein 31.1, Calcium 96 ½, Iron 5.95 ½,
Vitamin A 5,640, Thiamine .67 ½, Riboflavin .32 ½,
Vitamin C 26 ½, Niacin 4.4, Fatty Acids 35 ½

2nd Sunday Totals:
Calories: *1,416 ½*   Carbohydrates: *127 ½*

Supplements: For active non-dieting members of the family: *Breakfast:* an additional sausage, up to 3 pancakes with butter and syrup. *Lunch:* lettuce cups with the salmon; dark bread and butter; one or two glasses of whole milk. *Dinner:* a whole yam; more ham and beets if desired. Fruit and cheese with this dinner for dessert, using fresh fruit, if possible.

3RD MONDAY

Breakfast

Menu:	*Carbohyarates*
Corn Flakes, one medium bowl	24
Milk, ½ cup	6 ½
Raspberries, ¼ cup	21
Glass of Milk, low fat	13

Nutrients and Vitamins:

Protein 12 ½, Calcium 467, Iron .11 ½,
Vitamin A 59, Thiamine .27 ½, Riboflavin .71 ½,
Vitamin C 11 ½, Niacin .11 ½, Fatty Acids 0

Lunch

Menu:

Tomato Aspic
  with
Dilled Shrimp
Cottage Cheese
Coffee or Tea

Ingredients: *Carbohydrates*

Vegetable-tomato juice, 1 cup 10
Gelatin, ½ tablespoon 0
Celery, 1 stalk ....5 ½
Green onion, with part of green tops, 1 ....4 ½
Shrimp, 3 ounces 0
Yogurt, plain, 2 tablespoons ....1 ½
Dillweed, about 1 teaspoon 0
Cottage cheese, ½ cup 2
Rye or wheat bread, ½ slice 6
Butter, 1 teaspoon 0

Method:

Season and heat the tomato juice until gelatin is dissolved. Let cool and add the sliced onion and dethreaded celery. Pour ½ of the tomato mixture into a mold for a bottom layer. Let the mixture partially set. Mix drained shrimp with the yogurt and dillweed and spread over bottom layer. Add remaining tomato mixture for top layer and refrigerate until firm. The cottage cheese, seasoned, may be mounded on top to serve, or used as a "cottage-cheese patty melt" on the bread.

Nutrients and Vitamins:

Protein 37 ½, Calcium 247, Iron 4.4 ½,
Vitamin A 3,081, Thiamine .22 ½, Riboflavin .36 ½,
Vitamin C 44 ½, Niacin 4.3, Fatty Acids 10

Dinner

Menu:

Calf's Liver (or Baby Beef)
Piquant Sauce
Boiled Parsley Potatoes
Brussels Sprouts
Coleslaw with Pineapple and Dressing
Coffee or Tea

Ingredients:	*Carbohydrates*
Liver, 4 ounces	6
Piquant sauce, 1 tablespoon	4
Parsleyed potato, 1 medium	21
Brussels sprouts, ½ cup	6
Cabbage, ¼ small head	7
Pineapple, 1 slice	13
Coleslaw dressing, 4 tablespoons	2 ½

Method:

Melt a little butter (accounted for in liver computation) in skillet; roll to cover pan with very low heat.

Fry liver very slowly for extreme tenderness. Boil the potatoes and sprinkle with parsley and cook the brussels sprouts according to tape method. Grate the cabbage and mix with the pineapple cut into rather small sections. Add dressing (see Additional Recipes) and season a little more if desired.

Nutrients and Vitamins:

Protein 23, Calcium 184 ½, Iron 7.2,
Vitamin A 31,390, Thiamine .42, Riboflavin 3.27,
Vitamin C 127, Niacin 11.3 ½, Fatty Acids 11 ½.

3rd Monday Totals:
Calories *1,131*   Carbohydrates: *153*

Supplements: For active non-dieting members of the family: *Breakfast:* more of everything. *Lunch:* additional bread and butter; any dessert containing milk or cream. *Dinner:* soup, such as clam chowder or tomato (any soup containing milk). Larger servings of liver and vegetables; and for dessert: fruit and cheese, ice cream or a milk pudding.

3RD TUESDAY
Breakfast

Menu:	*Carbohydrates*
Vegetable-tomato Juice, ½ cup	6
Buckwheat Pancake, 1	6
Add Yogurt, 2 tablespoons and a pinch of Soda	2 ½
Poached or Soft-boiled Egg, 1	0
Glass of Milk, low fat	13

Nutrients and Vitamins:

Protein 20, Calcium 388, Iron 1.32 ½,
Vitamin A 2,280, Thiamine .28 ½, Riboflavin .74 ½,
Vitamin C 38, Niacin .13, Fatty Acids 8 ½

Lunch

Menu:

Tuna Stuffed Tomato
Cottage Cheese Patty Melt
   on Rye Bread
Crisp Celery and Green Olives
Coffee or Tea

Ingredients: *Carbohydrates*

Tomato, 1 medium 6
Tuna, 3 ounces, water packed 0
Celery, 1 stalk 1
Yogurt, plain, 4 tablespoons ....2 ½
Dillweed, about 1 teaspoon 0
Cottage cheese, ½ cup 2
Green olives, up to seven .... ½

Method:

See 1st Saturday lunch.

Nutrients and Vitamins:

Protein 40 ½, Calcium 193, Iron 3.0,
Vitamin A 1,827, Thiamine .18 ½, Riboflavin .45,
Vitamin C 39 ½, Niacin 11.82, Fatty Acids 11 ½

Dinner

Menu:

Pork Chops
  with
Steamed Cabbage
Corn
Fruit and Cheese
Coffee, Espresso or Tea

Ingredients: *Carbohydrates*

Pork chops, 1 large or 2 small 0
Steamed cabbage, 1 cup (or ⅓ small head) 9
Corn on the cob, 1 or kernal corn with butter
    or creamed corn, ½ cup 16
Fruit with cheese 10
Coffee or tea 0

Method:

Fry or bake chops as desired. Cut cabbage into wedges; season and steam in a little water in a heavy kettle with lid.

Nutrients and Vitamins:

Protein 26, Calcium 362 ½, Iron 3.0,
Vitamin A 1,025, Thiamine .80, Riboflavin .40,
Vitamin C 60 ½, Niacin 5.2 ½, Fatty Acids 39

3rd Tuesday Totals:
    Calories: *1,160*   Carbohydrates: *74 ½*

Supplements: For active non-dieting members of the family: *Breakfast:* more juice, pancakes and another egg, if desired, and syrup for the pancakes. *Lunch:*

pineapple or lettuce with the cottage cheese; more bread, or rolls and butter and a glass of whole milk. *Dinner:* greens; or spinach salad with crumbled bacon.

3RD WEDNESDAY
Breakfast

Menu: *Carbohydrates*

Tomato Juice, ½ cup 5
Chipped Dried Beef, ⅓ cup 0
Cream Cheese, 1 ½ ounces ....1 ½
Coffee or Tea 0

Method:

See 1st Tuesday breakfast.

Nutrients and Vitamins:

Protein 23, Calcium 46, Iron 3.10, Vitamin A 2,980, Thiamine .16, Riboflavin .32, Vitamin C 38, Niacin 3.2, Fatty Acids 12

Lunch

Menu:

Ham and Asparagus Supreme
  with
Cheddar Cheese Sauce
  on Toast Points
Pickled Peaches
Iced or Hot Coffee with Vanilla Ice Cream

Ingredients: *Carbohydrates*

Ham, 1 medium slice, precooked 0
Green asparagus, 6 spears 3
Cheddar cheese sauce, with nonfat milk,
  and chicken broth 3
Whole wheat bread, ½ slice ....: ∴6
Pickled peach, 1 whole 7
Vanilla ice cream, 1 tablespoon ....3 ½

Method:

See method for 1st Thursday for the Ham and Asparagus Supreme. Serve with pickled peach and coffee
with the ice cream.

Nutrients and Vitamins:

Protein 33.7, Calcium 68 ½, Iron 5.12 ½,
Vitamin A 1,720, Thiamine .55, Riboflavin .60 ½,
Vitamin C 17, Niacin 5.11 ½, Fatty Acids 29.5 ½

Dinner

Menu:

Oysters and Mushrooms
  with
Supreme Sauce
Spinach
Baked Julienne Carrots with Tarragon
Melon or other fresh fruit in season
Coffee or Tea

Ingredients: *Carbohydrates*

Oysters, 4 to 5 large, or 8 medium 4
Mushrooms, large, amount needed for oysters .....4 ½
Chicken broth, ½ cup 0
White wine, ¼ cup 0
Arrowroot, 1 teaspoon 1
Spinach, ½ cup 3
Carrots, about 20 thin strips (1 5 ½-inch carrot) 5
Melon, 1 good-sized wedge 9
Butter (for carrots) 1 teaspoon 0

Method:

If oysters are in jar or fresh: drain and reserve juice. Remove mushroom stems and mince. Place an oyster in each mushroom cap and place them in a shallow casserole with lid. Add the chicken broth, wine and mushroom stems; seal lid and bake for about 45 minutes in moderate oven. When mushrooms are done remove to warmed plate or platter and thicken the broth with arrowroot (or cornstarch), and pour over mushrooms and oysters. Cook the spinach using the tape method. Place the carrots in aluminum foil, dot with the butter and sprinkle with about ½ teaspoon tarragon and wrap to seal. Bake them along with the mushroom dish. If melon is not in season, serve a fruit that is, such as, ½ apple, a pear, 2 apricots, a peach, etc.

77

Nutrients and Vitamins:

Protein 17 ½, Calcium 289, Iron 7.88,
Vitamin A 23,880, Thiamine .36, Riboflavin .75 ½,
Vitamin C 66, Niacin 7.3, Fatty Acids 7 ½

3rd Wednesday Totals:
Calories: *958 ½*   Carbohydrates: *55 ½*

Supplements: For active non-dieting members of the family: *Breakfast:* more of the same. *Lunch:* ice cream, entire slice of bread. *Dinner:* soup; duchesse potatoes around mushroom-oyster platter, and cheese with fruit if melon is not served.

3RD THURSDAY

Breakfast

Menu: *Carbohydrates*

Orange Juice, ½ cup ....13 ½
Wheat Flakes, 1 medium bowl (1 ounce) 23
Strawberries, frozen ¼ cup 15
Milk, ½ cup ....6 ½

Nutrients and Vitamins:

Protein 9, Calcium 185 ½, Iron 2.3, Vitamin A 774,
Thiamine .32 ½, Riboflavin 13 ½, Vitamin C 70,
Niacin 2.4, Fatty Acids 0

Lunch

Menu:

Broiled Baked Ham and Swiss Cheese
  on Rye or Wheat Toast
String Bean and Onion Salad
  with
Vinagrette Dressing
Milk

Ingredients: *Carbohydrates*

Ham, three-ounce slice, without bone 0
Natural Swiss cheese, one-ounce slice 0
Rye or whole wheat bread, 1 slice 12
String beans, ½ cup 3
Onion, red or sweet white, ¼ medium size ....4 ½
Sugar, 1 teaspoon 6
Milk, low fat, 1 cup 13

Method:

See 2nd Wednesday lunch.

Nutrients and Vitamins:

Protein 39 ½, Calcium 639 ½, Iron 3.8, Vitamin A
1220, Thiamine .66 ½, Riboflavin 1.31,
Vitamin C 13 ½, Niacin 3.21 ½, Fatty Acids 50

79

Dinner

Menu:

Melon or Fresh Fruit Compote
Roasted Rock Cornish Game Hen
with
Spinach Soufflé Dressing
Cinnamon Apple Ring
Coleslaw with Dressing
Coffee or Tea

Ingredients: *Carbohydrates*

Melon or fresh fruit compote 9
Game hen, ½, without bones or skin 0
Spinach soufflé dressing, ½ cup 9
Velouté sauce, ⅓ cup 2
Cinnamon apple ring, 1 18
Cabbage, raw, ½ cup grated 2
Coleslaw dressing, ¼ cup 2½

Method:

Serve a fairly good-sized wedge of melon or use melon balls (frozen) or fresh fruit chipped up: a tablespoon of shredded coconut could be added here for orange sections since the calories are fairly low for this day. See Additional Recipes for velouté sauce and spinach dressing. As for the game hens: they are very good steamed as in 1st Sunday method, but are more attractive roasted, and just as good if kept covered lightly with aluminum foil and basted with the giblet broth rather frequently. Cook or bake for a good hour and a half, or until leg joint moves easily—time depends upon number cooking at one time. Use a moderate heat after pre-heating at 450°. Grate cabbage for coleslaw and see Additional Recipes for dressing.

Nutrients and Vitamins:

Protein 52, Calcium 294, Iron 7.9 ½,
Vitamin A 18,060, Thiamine .41, Riboflavin .83,
Vitamin C 124 ½, Niacin 22.26 ½, Fatty Acids 18 ½

3rd Thursday Totals:
Calories: *1,197 ½*   Carbohydrates: *139*

Supplements: For active non-dieting members of the family: *Breakfast:* simply more of everything. *Lunch:* pickled peach with open-faced sandwich; apple or other fruit pie for desert. *Dinner:* oven-browned potatoes, and any dessert containing milk or cheese.

3RD FRIDAY
Breakfast

Menu:	*Carbohydrates*
Grapefruit, fresh, ½ or frozen segments, ½ cup	14
Whole Wheat Toast, 1 slice	6
Soft-Boiled Egg, 1	0
Butter, 1 teaspoon	0

Nutrients and Vitamins:

Protein 8, Calcium 62, Iron 1.8 ½, Vitamin
A 1,060, Thiamine .13, Riboflavin .19 ½, Vitamin C
50, Niacin .5 ½, Fatty Acids 14 ½

Lunch

Menu:

Open Face Cheeseburger
Sliced Tomatoes
Green Olives
Milk

Ingredients: *Carbohydrates*

Ground lean beef, 3 ounces 0
Natural Cheddar cheese, 1 ounce 1
Wheat or rye bread, 1 slice 12
Tomato, 1 medium 6
Green olives, jumbo size, 3 .... ½
Milk, low fat, 1 cup (8 ounces) 13

Nutrients and Vitamins:

Protein 41 ½, Calcium 591, Iron 4.9 ½, Vitamin A
2,195, Thiamine .32, Riboflavin .72,
Vitamin C 37, Niacin 6.3, Fatty Acids 30 ½

Dinner

Menu:

Swordfish Provençale
    with
Tartar Sauce
Broccoli Amandine
French Fried Potatoes
Coffee or Tea

Ingredients: *Carbohydrates*

Swordfish, 6 ounces 0
Tartar sauce, 2 tablespoons ....2 ½
Broccoli, ½ cup 4
Slivered almonds, 1 teaspoon 2
French fried potatoes, frozen, 10 pieces 15

Nutrients and Vitamins:

Protein 55 ½, Calcium 260, Iron 4.6 ½, Vitamin A
5,052 ½, Thiamine 1.05 ½, Riboflavin .31 ½,
Vitamin C 66, Niacin 21.11, Fatty Acids 21 ½

Method:

See Additional Recipes for swordfish and broccoli
recipes.

3rd Friday Totals:
    Calories: *1,167½*   Carbohydrates: *76*

Supplements: For active non-dieting members of the
family: *Breakfast:* 2 eggs; more toast and butter or
jelly or jam. *Lunch:* hamburger bun, condiments,
pickles, whole milk and sherbet. *Dinner:* soup: jellied madrilene or consommé; more broccoli with
sauce and almonds. Dessert could be apple brown
Betty or cheese cake with cherries.

3RD SATURDAY

Breakfast

Menu: *Carbohydrates*

Orange Juice, ½ cup ....13 ½
Strawberries, ¼ cup (frozen) 15
Wheat flakes, medium bowl (1 ounce) 23
Milk, ½ cup, low fat ....6 ½

Nutrients and Vitamins:

Protein 1, Calcium 185 ½, Iron 2.3,
Vitamin A 774, Thiamine .32 ½, Riboflavin .31 ½,
Vitamin C 70, Niacin 2.4, Fatty Acids 0

Lunch

Menu:

Open Face Corned Beef Sandwich
Dill Pickles
Caraway Coleslaw with Dressing
Milk

Ingredients: *Carbohydrates*

Corned beef, 3 ounces 0
Rye bread, 1 slice 12
Dill pickle, 1 large 3
Cabbage, ¼ small head, grated 7
Dressing for coleslaw, 4 tablespoons .... 2 ½
Milk, low fat, 1 cup 13

Method:

Place warmed corned beef on rye bread, with mustard. Grate cabbage rather finely; see Additional Recipes for dressing.

Nutrients and Vitamins:

Protein 38, Calcium 494, Iron 6.9,
Vitamin A 880, Thiamine .23, Riboflavin .91,
Vitamin C 60 ½, Niacin 3.36 ½, Fatty Acids 17

Dinner

Menu:

Shrimp Cocktail with Piquant Sauce
Tournedos with Mushrooms
Fresh Peas with Pearl Onions
Baked Winter Squash
Small Black Coffee

Ingredients:	*Carbohydrates*
Shrimp, 1 ½ ounces	0
Piquant sauce, 1 tablespoon	3
Tournedos 3, (½-inch-thick slices of fillet mignon, 1.8 ounces each)	0
Butter, 1 teaspoon	0
Mushrooms, 7 medium	3
Fresh or frozen peas, ½ cup	9 ½
Small pearl onions, 6	5
Baked winter squash, ½ cup	11 ½

Method:

Ask your butcher to cut slices from a lean fillet: either the mignon or the one taken from the sevenbone chuck steak cut which is cheaper. In either case, if cut about ½-inch thick they will weigh about 6 ounces for the three rounds. Fry the rounds in butter until medium rare (over low heat for tenderness); add the mushrooms, whole or sliced, sautéed, to the tournedos when half-way done. The peas should be cooked using the tape method with the pearl onions added, the squash should also be cooked by the sealing method with just salt and pepper, to taste, added. Piquant Sauce for the shrimp cocktail is in Additional Recipes, but use a base of chili sauce with your own use of condiments and a little celery, if desired.

Nutrients and Vitamins:

Protein 71 ½, Calcium 192 ½, Iron 11.5,
Vitamin A 7,525, Thiamine .73 ½, Riboflavin .92,
Vitamin C 37, Niacin 14.9, Fatty Acids 18 ½
3rd Saturday Totals:
Calories: *1,202* ½   Carbohydrates: *127* ½

Supplements: For active non-dieting members of the family: *Breakfast:* the wheat flakes (some brands) have niacin, vitamin C and other vitamins added. More of the quantities should be sufficient; serve whole instead of low-fat milk. *Lunch:* a "lid" on the sandwich, more coleslaw and ice cream or custard-type dessert. *Dinner:* a green vegetable-based soup; such as cream of asparagus; duchesse, mashed or baked potatoes, with butter; for dessert; cream cheese cake with cherries or pineapple (small wedge).

3RD SUNDAY
Breakfast

Menu:

Grapefruit Juice
Waffles
Strawberry Whip Topping
Coffee or Tea

Ingredients:	*Carbohydrates*

Grapefruit juice, ½ cup 16
Waffle, ½ (make with enriched flour) 14
Strawberries, ¼ cup 15
Yogurt, plain, 2 tablespoons .... 1 ½

Method:

Fold the yogurt into the strawberries for waffle topping. Serve the waffle on warmed plate.

Nutrients and Vitamins:

Protein 5 ½, Calcium 137 ½, Iron 1.13,
Vitamin A 190, Thiamine .13 ½, Riboflavin .31,
Vitamin C 69 ½, Niacin .4, Fatty Acids 4 ½

Lunch

Menu:

Cream of Tomato Soup
Open Face Grilled Cheese Sandwich
   with
Crisp Bacon
Green Olives
Milk

Ingredients:	*Carbohydrates*

Tomato soup, with nonfat dried milk mixture
   added, ½ cup 9
Cheddar cheese, natural, mild or sharp, 1 ounce 1
Wheat bread, 1 slice 12
Bacon, 2 slices 0
Green olives, 7 .... ½
Milk, low fat, 1 cup (8-ounce glass) 13

Method:

Mix soup according to suggestions on can, but use a blend of nonfat dried milk and water, instead of regular milk. (Nonfat dried milk contains about 1,000 miligrams more of calcium than regular whole milk.) Place bread, lightly toasted, and cheese under broiler to desired degree of melt; add crisp bacon, blotted dry, on top of the melted cheese and toast. Serve with the soup, olives and milk.

Nutrients and Vitamins:

Protein 23 ½, Calcium 551, Iron 1.55,
Vitamin A 1,090, Thiamine .92 ½, Riboflavin .57,
Vitamin C 9, Niacin .56, Fatty Acids, 23 ½

Dinner

Menu:

Broiled Breast of Chicken Marinade
Italian String Beans
Potatoes Au Gratin
Fruit and Cheese
Coffee or Espresso

Ingredients: *Carbohydrates*

Chicken breasts, 6 ounces, without bone and skin .. 0
Italian string beans, fresh or frozen, ½ cup 3
Potatoes au gratin .... 14 ½
Fresh fruit, ½ piece (the carbohydrates allowance
    is an average of all fruits) .... 12 ½
Natural Swiss cheese (Gruyère or other), 1 ounce .. 1

Method:

See Additional Recipes for chicken and potato dishes. Cook beans using tape or foil method.

Nutrients and Vitamins:

Protein 53 ½, Calcium 421 ½, Iron 3.0 ½, Vitamin A 940, Thiamine .71 ½, Riboflavin .59, Vitamin C 37, Niacin 24.4, Fatty Acids 12 ½

Supplements:

For active non-dieting members of the family: *Breakfast*: more of everything and an egg or two. *Lunch*: a full 8 ounces of soup; another slice of toast for the sandwich and whole milk. *Dinner*: split pea or fresh pea soup with milk base; tossed green salad with Italian dressing.

3rd Sunday Totals:
Calories: *1,240*   Carbohydrates: *113*

Medically Approved Crash Diet

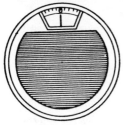

MEDICALLY APPROVED
CRASH DIET

The following "crash diet" was compiled and
tested by the author and follows the guidelines of doctors well-known in the field of nutrition and weight
control. Throughout, the carbohydrate count is low
and the protein, vitamin and calcium count is high.
Thus it is considered a "safe" crash diet, by the doctors
consulted, for a period of *nine* days. The diet could be
used up to fourteen days, the doctors felt, depending
upon the condition of the patient, his medical need to
lose weight and if he leads a fairly sedentary life.

The author had a physical examination on a
Tuesday; started the crash diet the next day and re-
ported back for an examination the following Thursday—9 days later. She lost 7 pounds. Her doctor then
advised a computed diet which was designed to help

her lose 2 to 3 pounds per week until 15 more pounds were lost. After, the computed diet would be retained with supplements to keep in trim. She was to weigh herself each day and if a pound was gained she omitted the supplements until it was lost.

The daily menus can be altered for reasons of economy, freshness of produce and family preferences. There are no variety meats included. No veal, ham, lamb, pork or turkey—just fish, chicken and steak, ground or regular (but always lean). If you live alone you may wish to eat the shrimp, tuna and lobster two days in succession, so they won't stand too long in the refrigerator. However, do follow each day's menu exactly as planned.

1ST DAY

Breakfast

	Calories	Carbohydrates
Tomato juice, 3 ounces	17	3.1
Melba toast, wheat, 1 slice	16	3.0
Soft boiled egg, 1	81	.4
Coffee, plain, or tea with lemon	2	0.

Lunch

	Calories	Carbohydrates
Lobster, broiled tails, 3 ounces	72	.7
Green asparagus spears, 6	20	3.3
Artichoke hearts *with*	22	4.9
Sour cream dressing (see Additional Recipes), 1 tablespoon	7	1.6

Dinner

	Calories	Carbohydrates
Ground round steak, seasoned; broiled		
4 ounces	250	0.
Spinach, 1 cup (use tape method)	42	6.3
Tomato, sliced, ½ with	30	6.0
Sour cream dressing, 2 tablespoons		
(see Additional Recipes)	14	3.2
Brussels sprouts	60	5.7

1st Day Total:
Calories: *633*   Carbohydrates: *38.2*

2ND DAY

Breakfast

	Calories	Carbohydrates
Corn flakes, 1 cup	81	18.4
Milk, low fat, 3 ounces (about ½ cup)	28	5.0
Apricots, canned in light syrup, 2 halves		
cut up (over corn flakes)	30	8.0

Lunch

	Calories	Carbohydrates
Tuna, 3 ounces, water pack, white		
albacore	100	0.
Cottage cheese, ⅓ cup	74	2.0
Tomato juice, 3 ounces	17	3.1
Dill pickle, 1 large	12	2.0

Drain and flake tuna. Add to cottage cheese and season to taste with a small amount of snipped parsley, Worcestershire sauce and pepper. Stir thoroughly. This and most of the crash diet menus sound bleak; but, not so!

It is surprising how good this tastes, and how it fulfills the appetite demands—one feels almost stuffed, and the dill picked is a perfect accompaniment.

Dinner

	Calories	Carbohydrates
Breast of chicken, broiled, 4 ounces, skinned	150	0.
Broccoli, 1 cup (use tape method)	45	6.7
Topping for broccoli, 2 tablespoons (see Additional Recipes)	14	3.2

2nd Day Total:
Calories: *551*   Carbohydrates: *48.4*

3RD DAY

Breakfast

	Calories	Carbohydrates
Soft boiled egg, 1	81	.4
Melba toast, 1 slice, wheat or rye	16	3.0
Tomato juice, 3 ounces	17	3.1

Lunch

	Calories	Carbohydrates
Shrimp, drained, 3 ounces	99	0.
Cottage cheese, ⅓ cup	74	.2
Melba toast, 1 slice	16	3.0
Dill pickle, large 1	12	2.0

See Menu #2 about mixing shrimp with the cottage cheese.

Dinner

	Calories	Carbohydrates
Salmon fillet, 3 ½ ounces; remove skin after broiling	140	0.
Spinach, ⅓ cup (use tape method)	14	2.1
Lettuce leaves, 6	30	2.6
Tomato, ½ large	30	6.0
Herbed seasoned dressing, ⅓ cup (see Additional Recipes)	45	3.6
Carrot sticks, 6 to 10 thin	20	4.8

Tear lettuce leaves into bite-sized pieces; cut the tomato in small wedges. Toss and cover with the dressing. Salmon should be seasoned to taste before broiling. To broil: place in aluminum foil with all edges curled up. This method keeps fish quite moist with more vitamins intact.

3rd Day Total:
  Calories: *594*   Carbohydrates: *28.4*

4TH DAY

Breakfast

	Calories	Carbohydrates
Corn flakes, 1 cup	81	18.4
Milk, low fat, 3 ounces	28	5.0
Strawberries, whole, 2 ounces, sliced, 1	50	6.0
Coffee, black or tea with lemon	2	0.

Lunch

	Calories	Carbohydrates
Shrimp, 3 ounces, drained	99	0.
Cottage cheese, ⅓ cup	74	.2
Tomato, ½ large	30	6.0

See Menu #2 for mixing cheese and shrimp. Garnish with tomato wedges. Season to taste.

Dinner

	Calories	Carbohydrates
Rock cornish game hen, skinned, ½	150	0.
Broccoli, 1 cup	45	6.7
Topping for broccoli, 2 tablespoons (see Additional Recipes)	14	3.2
Apple, baked, ½	33	8.7

Prepare game hen for baking; pare and peel one large apple, cooking type, cut in wedges. Season with seasoned salt and stuff hen. Cover lightly with aluminum foil except for the last ten minutes; baste fairly frequently with chicken broth supplied by cooking the neck and giblets. Cook the broccoli by the tape method and serve the topping at table. Reserve the other half of game hen for next day's dinner.

4th Day Total:
    Calories: *606*   Carbohydrates: *54.2*

5TH DAY

Breakfast

	Calories	Carbohydrates
Corn flakes, 1 cup	81	18.4
Milk, low fat, 3 ounces	28	5.0
Apricots, 2 halves, cut up (light syrup pack)	30	8.0

Lunch

	Calories	Carbohydrates
Tuna, water packed, white albacore, 3 ounces	100	0.
Cottage cheese, ⅓ cup	74	.2
Tomato juice, 3 ounces	17	3.1

Drain tuna and flake; mix about ½ teaspoon of dill with fish and let stand a little while. Mix with cottage cheese; serve with tomato juice.

Dinner

	Calories	Carbohydrates
Rock cornish game hen, skinned, ½	150	0.
Apple, baked, ½	33	8.7
String beans, French cut, 1 cup	25	6.6
Almonds, slivered, 1 teaspoon	23	1.0

Discard remainder of apple in ½ the game hen and use ½ of a fresh apple before reheating. Reheat in a sealed pot for about 45 minutes in a preheated 400° oven. Add broth and a little water or white wine before reheating.

5th Day Total:
    Calories: *561*   Carbohydrates: *51.0*

6TH DAY

Breakfast

	Calories	Carbohydrates
Corn flakes, 1 cup	81	18.4
Milk, low fat, 3 ounces	28	5.0
Apricots, 2 halves, cut up (light syrup pack)	30	8.0

Lunch

	Calories	Carbohydrates
Shrimp, drained, 3 ounces	99	0.
Cottage cheese, ⅓ cup	74	.2
Dill pickle, 1 large	12	.2

Dinner

	Calories	Carbohydrates
Fillet of sole, 2, broiled with lemon slices and white wine	88	0.
Tartar sauce, 2 tablespoons	30	3.0
String beans, French cut, 1 cup	25	6.6
Jello, any flavor, ½ cup	88	18.6
Yogurt, plain, 2 tablespoons, mixed with raspberry or mint extract	25	3.0

Place sole in aluminum foil; curl up edges, season to taste and add lemon slices and white wine (about ⅛ cup). See Additional Recipes for yogurt-based tartar sauce. Cook string beans by the tape method. Make jello according to package directions, and top with yogurt.

6th Day Total:
Calories *580*   Carbohydrates: *63*

7TH DAY

Breakfast

	Calories	Carbohydrates
Soft broiled egg, 1 large	81	.4
Melba toast, wheat or rye, 1 slice	16	3.0
Tomato juice, 3 ounces	17	3.1

Lunch

	Calories	Carbohydrates
Lobster tails, broiled, 3 ounces	72	.7
Asparagus spears, green, 6	20	3.3
Artichoke hearts, drained, 3 *with*	22	4.9
Sour cream dressing, 1 tablespoon, (see		
Additional Recipes)	7	1.6

Dinner

	Calories	Carbohydrates
Ground lean steak, 4 ounces	250	0.
Brussels sprouts, 1 cup	60	5.7
Italian string beans, ½ cup	12	3.3
Piquant sauce, 2 tablespoons	42	3.3

Season ground beef to taste; broil. Cook brussels sprouts by the tape method. Add tarragon vinegar to sprouts, if desired. Cook Italian string beans by the tape method. Add a sprig or two of minced parsley, garlic salt and Worcestershire sauce to the piquant sauce (see Additional Recipes) and serve with meat.

7th Day Total:
    Calories: *599*   Carbohydrates: *29.3*

Additional Recipes

DIET SCALE

ADDITIONAL RECIPES

CHICKEN BROTH

5 pounds chicken
neck, wings, backs
and giblets
2 carrots, chopped
2 celery stalks with
leaves, chopped
1 onion, peeled
and quartered

1 turnip,
quartered
2 bay leaves,
torn
½ teaspoon thyme,
rosemary and basil
12 peppercorns
Salt

Put chicken parts in a five-quart kettle. Add carrots, celery, onion, turnip, peppercorns and salt to taste. Add about four quarts of water. Seal the lid and cook for at least five hours. Remove fat and refrigerate. Strain, discarding solids and place in jars to freeze or refrigerate. If kept in the refrigerator, the broth must be reboiled every three days. Many of the recipes in this book have enough giblets to make broth for a family of two or three but if the family is larger this recipe is more economical as well as more nutritional.

HERBED STEAMED CHICKEN

1 whole chicken, 3 to 3 ½ pounds	Chicken neck and giblets
2 medium carrots	Salt and pepper
1 large onion, cut in wedges	to taste

1 or 2 stalks celery, with some chopped leaves

Assemble a large kettle, good fitting lid and a pie tin that will fit within the kettle. (Providing you do not own a steamer.) Wash and prepare chicken, carrots, onions and giblets. Cut carrots and onions in about 3-inch pieces. Salt and pepper vegetables and inside of chicken; stuff both cavities with the carrots and onions and skewer closed. Put chicken neck and giblets in the kettle; add four cups water and the herbs and peppercorns as outlined in the recipe for Chicken Broth, plus the cut up celery. Invert the pie tin over the fluid (float it). Place the chicken on its side on the tin. Seal the lid on with aluminum foil or tape and steam chicken for about 2 ½ hours on low heat or until tender. Turn chicken on its other side once about halfway through cooking time. Drain broth, chill and remove all fat; the broth makes a roux or a velouté sauce to serve with the chicken and a few other dishes.

ROUX

Both the broth given above and the chicken broth recipe given earlier need to be reduced to make a good sauce or gravy. Reduce broth by boiling 1 cup down to about ⅔ cup, and thicken to a nice clear consistency with arrowroot or cornstarch. Serve hot with chicken, Spinach Soufflé Dressing and other dishes.

VELOUTE SAUCE

Make a roux; reduce heat until all boiling or bubbling subsides. Gently fold in plain yogurt, to achieve a creamy consistency, about the color of cream gravy. Do not boil, or even simmer, simply bring up heat to serving temperature or yogurt will curdle. Taste for any added seasoning needed.

SPINACH SOUFFLE DRESSING
(sufficient for 1 chicken)

2 cartons frozen chopped spinach, cooked sealed method with no water	14 Saltine crackers
	½ small can water chestnuts, sliced
	½ teaspoon nutmeg
	Pepper to taste
3 to 4 whole eggs	

Dash of seasoned salt

Using fine colander or sieve, press any remaining water out of the spinach. Beat the eggs and whip into the cooled spinach. Add crackers, crumbled rather finely, one at a time and keep stirring. Add water chestnuts, nutmeg and condiments. Stuff chicken cavities lightly since the soufflé must have room to swell and become light. Skewer the cavities closed thoroughly. If some dressing is left over, and there usually is, place in small casserole and bake for about 25 minutes to augment family servings. The above dressing will stuff two rock cornish game hens; doubled it will stuff one capon, and tripled it will stuff one turkey.

BROILED BREAST OF CHICKEN MARINADE
(serves 1)

1 chicken breast, 6 ounces (without bone or skin)	1 tablespoon soy sauce

Marinate chicken breast in soy sauce. Easiest method: place chicken breast in foil, crumple up edges around it; add soy sauce and turn about four times to marinate. Broil, 6 inches from heat in same foil and sauce, turning after ten to fifteen minutes depending upon broiler. No other seasoning is necessary, because it is as tender, juicy and delicious as could be desired.

PORK CHOPS
WITH STEAMED CARAWAY SAUERKRAUT

1 pork chop, large shoulder cut	½ medium onion Caraway seeds
Sauerkraut	

Braise chop in pan with salt over very low heat until golden on both sides. Slice onion in thin slices and separate the rings. Lace the caraway seeds through the sauerkraut along with brown sugar, if desired. Put sauerkraut in casserole with lid; add onion rings across top surface, then the pork. Seal container with foil and bake in moderate oven for about 45 minutes or until done.

BROILED HERBED GROUND BEEF
(serves 2)

4 or 5 sprigs snipped parsley	½ cup nonfat dried milk mixed
Garlic salt, basil, salt and pepper to taste	2 slices rye or wheat bread
6 ounces lean, ground round steak	1 medium onion

Mix the parsley and condiments with the meat. Add the milk gradually so that mixture will be stirred to a fluffy consistency. Lightly toast one side of the bread; heap mixture on untoasted side of slices and spread evenly to edges. Place on broiler rack. Peel the onion and cut 4 slices from center of onion, ⅜-inch thick. Spread a little mayonnaise over the slices; salt and pepper lightly and place on rack besides beef patties. Broil for 12 minutes or until toast edges are somewhat charcoaled. Remove and break onion slices into rings and serve over the beef and toast.

SWORDFISH PROVENCALE

Swordfish fillets   **Lime or lemon juice**
White wine

Place fish on aluminum foil and crumple edges up and around it to partially cover and hold juices from spilling. Slice a lime or lemon thinly and place on top of swordfish. Salt lightly; add enough white wine to come up halfway on the fish. Broil 6 inches from flame until fish looks white and flaky. Do not overcook. Pour any remaining sauce over the swordfish as it has a tendency to be rather dry. Serve with tartar sauce, if desired.

SCALLOPS NICOLE IN WINE SAUCE

6 or 7 scallops   **1 teaspoon arrow-**
1 tablespoon butter   **root or 2 teaspoons**
¼ cup white wine   **cornstarch**
Juice of ½ lemon

Sauté scallops in butter on both sides until slightly golden. Add wine. Place lid on skillet and cook for 3 minutes. Squeeze the lemon juice over the scallops and remove them to a warm platter (keep in warm oven while making sauce). Stir a little water into arrowroot and add to wine and butter. Stir and heat until quite hot and thick. Pour over scallops. Sprinkle with parsley and serve.

POTATOES AU GRATIN
(serves 1)

½ cup sliced potatoes	Nonfat dried milk,
⅓ onion, thinly sliced	mixed with water
Salt and pepper	Paprika
to taste	

Make layers of potatoes, then onions and salt and pepper. Fill casserole within an inch of top; dust heavily with paprika after filling the dish with the milk mixture. Seal with aluminum foil or tape; bake in moderate oven about 45 minutes or until potatoes are quite tender. Remove lid last 10 minutes to crust top.

BOILED PARSLEY POTATOES

2 medium potatoes	4 sprigs parsley,
1 teaspoon salt	finely snipped
1 teaspoon butter	Salt and pepper
	to taste

Peel and quarter potatoes. Boil in water with the teaspoon of salt until tender, about 20 minutes; drain. Melt butter and add parsley and condiments; pour the parsley sauce over the potatoes and turn them to cover.

BAKED CARROTS WITH TARRAGON
(serves 2 to 3)

4 to 5 medium carrots	1 scant teaspoon
2 teaspoons butter	dried tarragon
Salt and pepper to taste	

Pare or scrape carrots and cut diagonally into about 3-

inch-long pieces; or cut into slender julienne strips. Place on 12-inch square of aluminum foil. Fold foil around with end edges folded to make a secure, leak-proof wrap. Bake approximately 1 hour and 15 minutes.

CROOKNECK YELLOW SQUASH WITH CHICKEN BROTH
(serves 1)

Crookneck squash, 1 whole (do not peel)   **½ cup chicken broth**
Dash salt and pepper

Trim off stem of squash; wash squash thoroughly and scrape off any discolored spots. Steam whole in chicken broth in pan with sealed lid, over low heat for about 45 minutes or less, depending upon altitude. Time may be shortened if heat is raised to medium low. (The skin of squash is as tender as the inside, and the taste of the squash left in its entirety is most delicious.)

STRING BEAN AND ONION SALAD
(serves 1)

½ carton frozen French cut string beans   **¼ medium sweet red or white onion, cut in thin rings**
1 teaspoon salad oil   **½ teaspoon sugar**
1 teaspoon garlic-flavored wine vinegar   **Dash of garlic salt, seasoned salt and seasoned pepper**

Cook string beans by the sealed method (aluminum foil here is good, because the beans are best in the salad if quite crisp). Add the rest of the ingredients and let marinate while preparing remainder of luncheon or dinner. Serve with marinade in salad bowls.

SLICED CUCUMBERS AND DRESSING
(serves 4 to 6)

2´ medium cucumbers, thinly sliced	¼ cup plain yogurt
1 sweet onion, thinly sliced	Salt and pepper to taste
1½ teaspoon salt	Few dashes paprika
1 teaspoon dillweed	2 large tomatoes (cut in wedges)

Mix cucumbers with onion slices and condiments with the yogurt. Refrigerate until ready to serve. Place cucumber mixture on center of serving bowl or plate; surround with tomato wedges for nondieting members of family.

TOPPING FOR BROCCOLI

1 tablespoon sour cream	Lemon or lime juice to taste
1 tablespoon yogurt	Garlic salt and Worcestershire sauce to taste

Mix and serve dollop fashion on top of broccoli or in bowl if several servings are desired.

COTTAGE CHEESE SALAD DRESSING
(serves 1)

½ cup cottage cheese   1 teaspoon snipped
1 tablespoon catsup   parsley
1 tablespoon oil   ¼ teaspoon paprika
1 tablespoon garlic   Dash of garlic salt
   wine vinegar   and seasoned salt

Stir all of the ingredients into the cottage cheese to blend well. Serve over lettuce wedges, or torn lettuce and tomato wedges.

SOUR CREAM SALAD DRESSING
WITH CAPERS
(enough for 2 salads)

2 tablespoons sour   ½ teaspoon sugar
   cream   Dash of pepper
2 tablespoons yogurt   3 sprigs of parsley,
1 tablespoon wine   finely snipped
   vinegar   1 tablespcon capers
¼ teaspoon each salt and seasoning salt

Blend sour cream and yogurt and mix in other ingredients. Let stand for an hour or two before serving over salads, tomatoes or vegetables as a topping.

HERBED SEASONED YOGURT DRESSING

⅓ cup yogurt
1 green onion, including green tops

Pinch each of crushed basil and thyme
Dash of Worcestershire sauce

3 or 4 sprigs snipped parsley

Mix ingredients thoroughly. Chill and serve over salads.

COLESLAW DRESSING
(serves 3 or 4)

½ cup evaporated milk
1 tablespoon cider or pear vinegar
1 teaspoon granulated sugar

½ teaspoon dry mustard
½ teaspoon cummin
Salt and pepper to taste
1 teaspoon celery seeds

Whip or beat all ingredients until the dressing is fairly thick. Chill and serve, mixed thoroughly, on grated cabbage.

Caraway Seed Coleslaw Dressing:

Add about 2 teaspoons caraway seeds to above recipe and let dressing stand for several hours, stirring occasionally.

ARTICHOKE DRESSING
(serves 4 to 5)

2 hard-boiled eggs	**¼ teaspoon Wor-**
½ cup mayonnaise	**chestershire sauce**
½ cup yogurt	**1 tablespoon dill-**
¼ teaspoon dry	**weed**
mustard	**Salt and pepper**
	to taste

Paprika for garnish

Mash up the eggs to a paste; add all the rest of the ingredients and stir thoroughly. Chill for an hour or so, and garnish with paprika. Serve in individual bowls for dipping or stuff artichokes with dressing after trimming tops.

PIQUANT SAUCE
(serves 2)

4 tablespoons chili	**½ teaspoon Worces-**
sauce	**tershire sauce**

1 tablespoon finely snipped parsley

Mix and serve at once to prevent the parsley wilting.

CHIVE CREAM TOPPING

Mix equal amounts of sour cream and yogurt. Add chopped green chives, seasoned salt and seasoned pepper to taste.

CREAM OF HORSERADISH SAUCE
(makes 1 ½ cups; may be refrigerated)

½ cup sour cream	1 teaspoon salt
½ cup plain yogurt	¼ teaspoon sweet
½ cup hot or medium	basil
hot horseradish	½ teaspoon grated
1 tablespoon Dijon	lemon rind
mustard	

Combine sour cream and yogurt, blend well. Add the remaining ingredients and stir thoroughly. Let stand after mixing in the refrigerator for an hour or two before serving.

TARTAR SAUCE I
(makes 1 ½ cups; may be refrigerated)

½ cup mayonnaise	1 tablespoon fresh
½ cup yogurt,	dill
plain	1 tablespoon
2 tablespoons	chopped parsley
chopped chives	1 teaspoon lemon
	juice

Stir ingredients together thoroughly, place in jar with lid.

TARTAR SAUCE II
(serves 2)

2 tablespoons mayonnaise

2 tablespoons yogurt, plain

1½ teaspoons sweet pickle, chopped fine

½ teaspoon capers

1 teaspoon green onion tops, chopped fine

½ teaspoon Worcestershire sauce

¼ teaspoon seasoning salt

Blend mayonnaise and yogurt together; add rest of ingredients and stir thoroughly. Actually this sauce can be used with any fish that is broiled or breaded and thus fairly dry.

INDEX

A

Additional recipes, 101-115
Apricot sauce, 68
Artichoke dressing, 113
Asparagus, ham and,
supreme, 35, 75
Avocado, stuffed, with
shrimp salad, 58

B

Bacon, grilled cheese and,
on toast, 45, 87
Baked carrots with
tarragon, 36, 76, 108
Baked ham with apricot
sauce, 68
Beef:
broiled herbed ground,
60, 106
dried chipped with cream
cheese, 28, 48, 75
ground steak a la Scotch
grill, 31
steak châteaubriand, 42
tournedos with
mushrooms, 85
Beets, sliced with onion
rings, 68
Boiled parsley potatoes, 59,
71, 108

Braised lamb chops, 32
Broccoli, topping for, 32, 95,
97, 110
Broiled baked ham, and
Swiss cheese, 54, 79
Broiled herbed ground
beef, 60, 106
Broiled breast of chicken
marinade, 52, 88, 105
Broth, chicken, 102
Buckwheat pancakes with
yogurt, 40, 53, 66, 72

C

Cabbage, steamed knock-
wurst with, 49
Caraway sauerkraut,
steamed, with pork chops,
59, 105
Caraway seed coleslaw
dressing, 46, 84, 112
Carrots, baked, with
tarragon, 36, 76, 108
Cheddar cheese sauce, 35, 75
Cheese, grilled and bacon on
toast, 45, 87
Chicken:
broiled breast of,
marinade, 52, 88, 105
broth, 102
herbed steamed, 38, 103
livers sauté, 44, 55

steamed, 46
Chicken broth, 102
Chicken livers sauté, 44, 55
Chipped beef, dried, with
cream cheese, 28, 48, 75
Chived cream topping, 64,
113
Coleslaw dressing, 71, 80,
112
Cottage cheese patty melt,
grilled, 38, 71, 73
Cottage cheese salad
dressing, 111
Cottage cheese, shrimp
and, 95, 97, 99
Cottage cheese, tuna fish
and, 94, 98
Crash diet, 91-100
explanation of, 92
Cream cheese, dried chipped
beef with, 28, 48, 75
Cream of horseradish
sauce, 51, 114
Crookneck yellow squash
with chicken broth, 39,
109
Cucumbers, sliced and
dressing, 52, 110

D

Dilled shrimp, tomato aspic
with, 70

Dill sauce and capers, 67
Dressings:
artichoke, 113
caraway seed coleslaw,
46, 84, 112
coleslaw, 71, 80, 112
cottage cheese salad, 111
herbed seasoned yogurt,
96, 112
Hungarian, 45
sour cream salad, with
capers, 93, 94, 100, 111
spinach soufflé, 46, 80,
104
Dried chipped beef with
cream cheese, 28, 48, 75

F

Filet of sole with champagne
sauce, 39
Fish:
pink salmon aspic, 28
pink salmon with dill
sauce and capers, 67
salmon fillet, 96
sole, filet of with cham-
pagne sauce, 39
swordfish provencale, 82,
107
tuna stuffed tomato, 41,
73

O

Onion rings, sliced beets with, 68
Onion, string bean and, salad, 54, 79, 109
Oysters and mushrooms with supreme sauce, 76

P

Pancakes, buckwheat, with yogurt, 40, 53, 66, 72
Parmesan cheese, thick boiled tomato slices with, 44
Peppers, green, a la Florentina, 26
Pineapple Russe, 32
Pink salmon aspic, 28
Pink salmon with dill sauce and capers, 67
Piquant sauce, 60, 61, 71, 85, 100, 113
Pork chops provencale, 36
Pork chops with steamed caraway sauerkraut, 59, 105
Potatoes au gratin, 88, 108
Potatoes, boiled parsley, 59, 71, 108

R

Recommended daily nutrient and vitamin allowances, 15
Roasted rock cornish game hen, 80
Rock cornish game hen with apple, 97, 98
Roux, 104

S

Salads:
  lobster, 48
  sliced beets with onion rings, 68
  sliced cucumbers and dressings, 52, 110
  string bean and onion, 54, 79, 109
Salmon fillet, 96
Sauces:
  apricot, 68
  cheddar cheese, 35, 75
  cream of horseradish, 51, 114
  dill, and capers, 67
  piquant, 60, 61, 71, 85, 100, 113
  supreme, 76
  tartar I, 114

tartar II, 82, 99, 115

veloutè, 46, 80, 104

Sauerkraut, steamed caraway, with pork chops, 59, 105

Scallops nicole in wine sauce, 61, 107

Scrambled eggs with Swiss cheese, 57

Scrambled eggs with yogurt, 37

Shrimp and cottage cheese, 95, 97, 99

Shrimp, dilled, tomato aspic with, 70

Shrimp salad, avocado stuffed with, 58

Sliced beets with onion rings, 68

Sliced cucumbers and dressing, 52, 110

Sour cream and yogurt topping, 28

Sour cream salad dressing with capers, 93, 94, 100, 111

Spinach soufflé dressing, 46, 80, 104

Squash, crookneck yellow, with chicken broth, 39, 109

Steak châteaubriand, 42

Steak, ground, a la Scotch grill, 31

Steamed caraway sauerkraut, with pork chops, 59, 105

Steamed chicken, 46

Steamed knockwurst with cabbage, 49

Strawberry whip topping, 86

String bean and onion salad, 54, 79, 109

Stuffed avocado with shrimp salad, 58

Stuffed tomato, with tuna, 41, 73

Supreme sauce, 76

Swiss cheese, broiled baked ham with, 54, 79

Swiss cheese, scrambled eggs with, 57

Swordfish provencale, 82, 107

T

Table of vegetables and water needed to cook, 20

Tape method for cooking vegetables, 18

Tarragon, baked carrots with, 36, 76, 108

Tartar sauce I, 114

Tartar sauce II, 82, 99, 115

Thick broiled tomato slices with Parmesan cheese, 44

Tomato aspic with dilled shrimp, 70